The Shape of Our Lives

Study One in The Ekklesia Project's
Getting Your Feet Wet Series

Philip D. Kenneson
Debra Dean Murphy
Jenny C. Williams
Stephen E. Fowl
James W. Lewis

WIPF & STOCK · Eugene, Oregon

THE SHAPE OF OUR LIVES

ISBN 13: 978-1-60608-054-2

www.wipfandstock.com

About The Ekklesia Project

The Ekklesia Project is a network of Christians from across the Christian tradition who rejoice in a peculiar kind of friendship rooted in our common love of God and the Church. We come together from Catholic parishes, Protestant congregations, communities in the Anabaptist tradition, house-churches and more as those who are convinced that to call ourselves 'Christian' means that following Jesus Christ must shape all areas of life. Seeing Christ's Body as our "first family," the Ekklesia Project aims to put discipleship and the Church as an alternative community of practices, worship, and integration at the center of contemporary debates on Christianity and society.

For more information about The Ekklesia Project, see its website: www.ekklesiaproject.org

About the Congregational Formation Initiative

The overarching goal of The Ekklesia Project's Congregational Formation Initiative (CFI) is to develop creative and effective ways of supporting congregations that are committed to making lifelong formation and discipleship central to their life together. To support this goal, the CFI fosters collaboration among pastors, scholars and lay persons to develop, refine and disseminate resources and processes that will help initiate and sustain congregational conversations about the fundamental identity and mission of the church. For more information about CFI, including the place of this study in the overall initiative, see the EP website listed above.

All scripture quotations in the following study are from the New Revised Standard Version unless otherwise noted.

Manufactured in the U.S.A.

TABLE OF CONTENTS

Introduction to the "Getting Your Feet Wet" Series

What's this all about?

The first two studies in the "Getting Your Feet Wet" series are designed to foster important conversations within the life of congregations and parishes. They begin with the assumption that the church in our day needs to think carefully and discuss openly what it means to be the church. Just as it's difficult to imagine that a business, school or athletic team could accomplish its purpose if participants had very different and possibly competing understandings of what that purpose was, so it is with the church. If the church gathers each week with vastly different and competing understandings of what it means to be the church, it's hard to imagine that things will go well.

These first two studies, therefore, focus on two important issues. The first study, "The Shape of Our Lives," explores the many ways in which formation is always happening whether we are aware of it or not. This study's guiding assumption is twofold: first, that the church is called to be a community of formation; and second, that this calling is always lived out in particular social contexts where other kinds of formation are also taking place. Are we aware of how our lives are being shaped simply by living everyday life in the ways we are encouraged to do? Are we aware of the ways that the cultural formation we undergo may be at odds with our call to be formed into the image of Christ? It's one thing, of course, to *acknowledge* that we are always being shaped and formed by the world around us; it's quite another to consider deeply how this may be taking place in very particular ways in our daily lives.

Once we are clearer about the particular ways in which formation happens, we are in a better position to discuss the matters raised in the second study, "The Shape of God's Reign." In this second study, the central questions are these: What do we think the purpose of the church is and where did our notions about this come from? Is it possible that our host culture has shaped us to think about the church in ways that are unhelpful if not unfaithful? What is God doing in the world and how have we as the church been called to participate with God in that work? These are weighty matters indeed, but we take them up not primarily as matters of intellectual curiosity, but as a means of discerning where God is at work in our lives and where further growth and maturity might be required.

A different kind of study

Both of these studies are designed to encourage congregations to develop or strengthen habits of attending carefully to their life together. As you are probably aware, you can tell a great deal about a congregation by examining its conversational habits. When people in a congregation get together, *what* do they talk about? Are they able to talk about things that really matter (and are therefore potentially "dangerous"), or is all or most of their conversation about safe things such as the weather and sports? And if a congregation *has* developed the habit of talking about important but difficult matters, *how* are these conversations carried out? Is there anything about the way Christians engage in difficult conversations that is rooted in our vision of the church, or do we go about these conversations largely as the surrounding culture does?

Because many congregations need to learn how to engage in serious conversation, these studies are designed more as an aid to important and potentially defining conversations than they are as a delivery system for particular content. Or put differently, the primary focus of these studies is not the words on the page, but your life together as a congregation. Your congregational life, if you will, is the "text" under consideration. For this reason when you come to the end of these studies, the ways you have learned to be in conversation together will be more important than the study materials themselves. In at least one important respect, then, these studies will never be "over," because once you develop the habit of taking seriously the shape of your life together, you can never stop doing so.

It may be helpful to think of the following pages as a kind of scaffolding. Of course scaffolding is only a tool—and a rather mundane tool at that—but it can at times be indispensable. If you've ever needed stable footing for accessing hard-to-reach areas, either to examine a structure or to engage in needed repairs, you know how important scaffolding can be. But even in those instances, the scaffolding isn't the focus of the construction project; it's simply a tool to aid in the necessary work. We would grow concerned if the construction workers gathered every week just to discuss their opinions about the scaffolding. In the same way, you may need to remind yourselves periodically that these pages aren't the focus of your study; they are offered only as an aid to help you discern some important things about your life together. Of course, important congregational work can be done (and should be done) without the aid of this scaffolding. Indeed, there's certainly no reason to think that every congregation will either need this tool or use it in the same way. Whether and how it will be used will depend on the kind of work the Spirit is already doing in your congregation.

For this reason, the pages that follow are meant to assist in shared exploration, not to set a one-size-fits-all agenda. No one expects that when you complete these studies you will have all the answers; rather, the hope is that you will have discovered together the importance of several defining questions around which you may orient your continuing journey to be a faithful community of disciples of Jesus Christ.

Some working assumptions

All of us have working assumptions that guide nearly everything we do. Sometimes we're quite conscious of these assumptions, though often we're not. You may find it helpful to know upfront some of the key working assumptions behind this series. Although there's no expectation that you will necessarily share all of these assumptions, the hope is that by the time the studies are completed you will at least see why some of these assumptions might matter.

Here are a few important ones:

◆ The Christian faith is not simply a set of beliefs or doctrines that one assents to with one's mind, but an entire way of life animated by the Spirit of Jesus Christ.

◆ The church is a community of disciples called together to bear embodied witness to Jesus Christ, not least by being formed more and more into the image of Christ.

◆ Christian formation is always enabled and empowered by the Holy Spirit, yet it typically takes place through rather mundane human processes and activities.

- None of us has arrived; we are all pilgrims on the path of discipleship to fullness of life in Jesus Christ.

- Despite very real challenges and obstacles, the church in our day has good reasons to believe that God's Spirit is alive and working in and through our congregations.

Worries about "formation" language

In our day, no discussion of "formation" can take place very long before some people get at least a little nervous. Is someone going to dictate what the shape of our lives is to be? Is someone going to suggest that faithfulness to Christ has to look one particular way? Isn't there a real danger when people presume to form others?

In broaching this topic, we do well to avoid two extremes. At one extreme is what we might call the "cookie-cutter" approach. This approach to formation insists that it's relatively easy to spot the "real Christians" because they're the ones engaging in the behaviors that "real Christians" engage in and avoiding the behaviors that "real Christians" are supposed to avoid. With this approach, formation primarily involves making sure everyone understands which behaviors are to be embraced and which ought to be avoided. In some circles, for example, real Christians are those who go to church every Sunday and who don't go to R-rated movies.

At the other extreme is what we might call the "hands-off" approach. This approach insists that very little, if anything, can or should be said definitively about the shape of Christian life. With this approach, any attempt to form people intentionally is regarded as an unwarranted imposition on people's freedom to shape their own personhood.

To its credit, the cookie-cutter approach rightly senses that we ought to be able to say *something* about how our lives should be affected by the good news of Jesus Christ. Is there really *no* reference point at all, no way to discern whether a particular person or community of persons is becoming more or less conformed to the image of Christ?

To *its* credit, the hands-off approach is nervous about the ways in which this reference point has been named in the past. Some churches have too often given the impression that "real" Christians are simply those who avoid certain kinds of behaviors. And too often these lists of taboo behaviors have little connection to the good news of Jesus Christ. (The release of the film "The Passion of the Christ" led some churches, for example, to re-examine their blanket prohibition against R-rated movies and to admit that a more nuanced form of discernment might be needed in the church about such matters.)

Although on the surface these two extremes appear to be polar opposites, on a deeper level they are remarkably similar in at least one important respect: they both largely presume that what it means to be a Christian is primarily an *individual* affair. In the cookie-cutter approach, the individual is told what behaviors he or she needs to engage in (and avoid) in order to be considered a faithful Christian. In the hands-off approach, individuals are largely left to their own devices to figure this out, since no one else would presume to tell them what their lives should look like.

This study begins with a different assumption: that what it means to be a Christian is first of all a communal affair. Indeed, one the primary purposes of this series of studies is to encourage congregations to develop more robust practices of communal discernment--to continually seek to understand how best to live out our shared calling to be a community of disciples in a particular time and place.

A couple of words about format

Because these studies are exploratory in character, they make extensive use of questions throughout. Please resist the temptation to think of the questions as supplementary. In fact, the relatively brief material that opens each session is offered primarily in order to aid what we hope is good discussion. This also means that you shouldn't panic if you don't completely understand something that you read in preparation for a given week's discussion; chances are that your understanding will be greatly enhanced after you've had an opportunity to discuss it together with others. Similarly, try not to be frustrated by the fact that more questions are provided than most groups will need; rather, simply focus on those questions (either a few of the ones provided or those arising out of your own group) that you think most important for exploring your life together.

You are encouraged to write down in the spaces provided your reflections about these and other questions that arise during your study. This study is intentionally printed with space for recording your own questions and for jotting down responses from others that come up in conversation.

Each session ends with a "paying greater attention" section that encourages you to continue to reflect on these matters in the course of your everyday life. You need not, of course, limit yourself to these suggestions; you're encouraged to think of more and better suggestions. The important point is to find specific ways and develop the regular habit of reflecting more intentionally upon the shape of your life and the formative influences upon it.

Hopes and expectations

Each group that takes up this study will no doubt have its own hopes and expectations as it begins these conversations. In fact, it would be wise to articulate as many of these as possible as you begin your study, in order to get a sense of what people hope will result from your time together. As a way of getting started with that conversation, here are a few things that those of us who wrote this guide hope will happen as a result of your time and commitment:

- That you will deepen your desire and your abilities to reflect on the shape of your own life and the life of your congregation.

- That you will deepen your desire and your abilities to discuss with other people matters that matter.

- That as a congregation you will develop a shared vocabulary as a tool to reflect upon and discuss together your common life.

♦ And finally, that your conversations together would be used by God in some small way to deepen your shared practice of living out the gospel of Jesus Christ in your corner of God's world.

Final words of wisdom

Congregations who have used these studies in the past have offered several words of wisdom for those taking up the challenge in their own contexts. Here is some of what they have offered:

♦ Be patient with all those involved in the study (including yourself!) and with the seemingly slow pace of congregational formation generally. Just as "Rome wasn't built in a day," neither are faithful congregations. The habits of thought and action that pose significant obstacles to faithful discipleship are firmly rooted in all of us as a result of years of formation. Examining these habits to discern how they are helping or hurting our life together as the church will require both time and a willingness to be uncomfortable. None of this will be easy, and there are no quick fixes or short cuts.

♦ Similarly, don't minimize what the Spirit may be *already* doing in your group as you gather to give careful consideration to your life together. Just because you don't see any tangible results right away doesn't mean that the Spirit isn't working in your common life. Each time you gather, devote some time to celebrating the places where you do see the Spirit working in your life together and continue to trust that God will bring to completion the good work begun in you.

♦ Finally, these studies are most beneficial when they are part of a larger practice of sharing life together. Many groups make these studies a part of a regular gathering where participants share a meal and their lives with each other. Much of the long term benefit from these studies comes from intentionally connecting with people in your congregation on a deeper level.

Conversation #1: Formation Happens!

> *O Lord, you are our Father;*
> *we are the clay, and you are our potter;*
> *we are all the work of your hand. (Isaiah 64:8)*
>
> *I appeal to you therefore, brothers and sisters, by the mercies of God, to present your bodies as a living sacrifice, holy and acceptable to God, which is your spiritual worship. Do not be conformed to this world, but be transformed by the renewing of your minds, so that you may discern what is the will of God—what is good and acceptable and perfect. (Romans 12:1-2)*
>
> *Don't let the world squeeze you into its mold. (Romans 12:2; J. B. Phillips)*

Whether we know it or not, or whether we acknowledge it or not, we are always being formed. We are always being molded. We are always being shaped. In short: formation happens.

In this respect, human beings are a bit like play-dough or silly putty: made in such a way that our lives are incredibly malleable, capable of being formed and shaped in any number of different ways. Presumably God could have created human beings less like play dough and more like rocks. Had God done so, we would have arrived on the scene in a far more fixed and finished state.

Now even though God made us capable of being shaped in any number of ways, this shouldn't be taken to imply that God doesn't care what shape we take. On the contrary, God desires that our lives take a certain shape, a certain form. Scripture tells us that God desires that our lives be

> **God desires that our lives be conformed to the image of Christ.**

conformed to the image of Christ (Rom. 8:29; 2 Cor. 3:18). Indeed, 2 Peter suggests that the ultimate goal of God's work in our lives is to enable us to be "partakers of the divine nature" (2 Pet. 1:4). In this important respect, therefore, all Christians have the same calling: to be conformed to the image of Christ. All of us have been called to have our lives shaped and formed according to the pattern we see in Jesus. C. S. Lewis once insisted that the church exists for no other reason than to form persons into "little Christs" (which is what the word "Christian" literally means, after all). Indeed, Lewis went on to insist that if the church is not doing this, then "all the cathedrals, clergy, missions, sermons, even the Bible itself, are simply a waste of time" (*Mere Christianity*, 199).

Yet as already suggested, God's desire is not simply *that* we be conformed to the image of Christ. If that was all that God desired, God could have created us as already finished sculptures. But God didn't do this, presumably because God desires that *we desire* to be so conformed and to open ourselves up to that transformation. God cannot force us to love God or to desire to be like God any more than one of us can force another person to love us or want to be like us. To coerce love is to violate its very nature. So Christian formation is first of all about right desire, about being open to the transformation that is possible in and through Jesus Christ and the work of the Spirit.

As the Body of Christ, the church is called to bear the imprint, the pattern, the image of Christ, just as a piece of play-dough held tightly in your palms bears the imprint, the pattern, the image of your hands. Now human formation is, of course, much more complicated than picking up a piece of play-dough and fashioning it into whatever strikes your fancy at the moment. Perhaps one of the most important differences is that our lives are being formed by many, many different factors. It's as if multiple hands are working on the ball of play-dough that is our life, often at the same time, and often with different purposes in mind. So if we feel as though our lives are being pulled and twisted in different directions, there's good reason for that: they *are* being pulled and twisted in different directions!

> ***Christian formation is first of all about right desire.***

Consider just one example. It seems rather obvious that one of the principle virtues of contemporary society is ambition. We are told in countless subtle and not-so-subtle ways that if you want to succeed in life, you have to order your life in such a way that you are always calculating how to get ahead, how to insure that you are constantly advancing toward the top. And so when we attend to these pressures—these hands on our lump of clay—we find ourselves being formed to think and act in certain ways. We are encouraged to think of our co-workers in certain ways; we are led to think of the purpose of our work in certain ways; we are even inclined to think of the direction and purpose of our entire lives in certain ways.

But what happens, however, when those of us who are being so formed gather as the church on a particular Sunday morning and hear the following scripture read:

> Do nothing from selfish ambition or conceit, but in humility regard others as better than yourselves. Let each of you look not to your own interests, but to the interests of others. (Philippians 2:3-4)

How are we supposed to negotiate these different expectations? How are we supposed to be formed into the image of the humble Christ when the world around us is trying to squeeze us into its "ambitious" mold? Now perhaps these seemingly different pressures, voices, and agendas can be brought together in such a way that we can have our ambition and exercise humility at the same time. Perhaps. But at the very least we should acknowledge that there is a tension here, that what we have is a situation about which most thoughtful Christians would likely feel conflicted, pulled as they are in very different directions.

Disciplined formation

Although formation happens whether we are aware of it or not, most of us rightly assume that formation of a particular kind or direction requires disciplined and sustained effort. If we desire to become an accomplished ballerina, baseball player, violinist or painter, we don't just sit around and hope that we will one day wake up and it will be so. Rather, we know that nothing short of years of disciplined and dedicated effort will be necessary if we are to have any hope of being so transformed. Similarly, year in and year out, parents make decisions about the formation of their children with the clear recognition that formation in a particular direction is not a matter of magic, but of disciplined and thoughtful action.

Yet why is it that all of us know that being an athlete or artist requires discipline, but many of us too often assume that being a follower of Jesus requires little or none? Why is it that none of us would be so naïve as to believe that we would simply wake up one day and be capable of playing the piano, yet many of us act as if the Christian life can be lived well without a similar intentionality?

For some of us this attitude stems, at least in part, from our fear that the Christian faith will be transformed into a form of "works-righteousness," by which we mean an attempt to earn God's favor through our actions. Of course we are right to insist, as does scripture, that our salvation is the result not of our works but of God's gracious initiative in and through Jesus Christ (Eph. 2:8-9). Yet such an affirmation of God's grace should not be taken to mean that our *response* to that grace is insignificant, for as Paul goes on to tell the Ephesians: "For we are what [God] has made us, created in Christ Jesus for good works, which God prepared beforehand to be our way of life" (Eph. 2:10). Christian formation is not, therefore, to be understood as an attempt to transform ourselves into "super-Christians" who can earn God's favor through good works; rather, Christian formation involves the slow process of being shaped by God's Spirit to daily present our entire lives to God as a "living sacrifice" in worshipful response to God's gracious initiative.

Of course, such "living sacrifices" are never offered in a cultural vacuum. This is why Christians must also pay careful attention to the cultures of formation within which they dwell.

The power of expectations

Now whatever else cultures are, they are complex formation systems that shape us with certain expectations. To be "at home" in a particular culture is to know what to expect. For example, if you find yourself "at home" in that subculture we call "the mall," it is because you have been formed in such a way that you have clear expectations about what kinds of things routinely happen there. As a result, you know what is expected of you and what you can expect of others in that particular setting.

The same could be said, of course, with respect to other subcultures as well. College professors often find, for example, that students have very specific expectations about what will happen during the first class session of a new term. They expect the professor to walk into class, introduce herself, welcome them to a new semester and a new class, read the roll, distribute and discuss the syllabus, give them their first assignment, and dismiss them early. (This last expectation is the strongest!)

Now where and how did these students learn these expectations? The students didn't come out of the womb with these expectations, nor did they ever take a course entitled, "What to Expect on the First Day of Class." What they *did* do, however, was

> ***Cultures are complex formation systems that shape us with certain expectations.***

thoroughly (and largely unconsciously) internalize a whole set of experiences such that certain kinds of behavior, certain ways of doing things, came to be seen as "normal" and therefore "expected."

Of course, shopping malls and college classrooms are not the only kind of subcultures with their own sets of expectations and definitions of "normal." We also speak about "corporate cultures" and "workplace cultures," which are every bit as formative for the way we see and experience our daily lives as any other. In these settings certain kinds of behaviors and attitudes are considered "normal" and so are therefore instilled largely through day-to-day participation in that culture.

If you have any doubts about the power of cultures to form expectations (and thus affect your comfort level), try to remember the last time you found yourself in a culture where you were *not* at home. (This might have been the result of traveling to a different country, or it may have involved simply stepping into an unfamiliar subculture closer to home.) Here's the question: What was it that made you feel "out of place" or "not at home"? For some, it will have been a different language, a different diet, or a different way of doing a routine activity (such as driving on the "wrong" side of the road). For others, it will have been some other clearly noticeable difference that made them less than fully comfortable.

Regardless of the specific differences, most people admit that what makes them most uneasy about being in a less-than familiar culture is the anxiety that accompanies not knowing what to expect. This anxiety is real whether you are stepping off the plane in another country, walking into an office on the first day of a new job, or slipping into the back row on your first Sunday at a new church. It's hard to relax if you're unsure about what is expected of you and about what you can expect of other people around you. Most of us find

> **Cultures influence the very way we see and interpret what's going on around us.**

it profoundly unsettling to always be wondering if something we are doing (or not doing) is unintentionally offending the sensibilities of those around us.

But cultural expectations do not merely affect our comfort level; they also influence the very way we see and interpret what's going on around us. Many first-century Jews, for example, had fairly specific expectations regarding God's promised and long-awaited Messiah. Thus, while some believed that Jesus was indeed the Messiah, others had deep misgivings rooted in their expectations of what the Messiah ought to "look like." Thus, when Philip tells Nathaniel that they have "found him about whom Moses in the law and also the prophets wrote, Jesus son of Joseph from Nazareth," Nathaniel replies: "Can anything good come out of Nazareth?" (John 1:45-46). In other words, Nathaniel's expectations about Messiah (and Nazareth) made it difficult for him to "see" Jesus as the Messiah. In a similar way, Peter's understanding of Messiah makes it difficult for him to hear and accept Jesus' teaching about his impending suffering and death (Matt. 16:21-23).

Each of us likewise interprets and evaluates countless experiences in our everyday lives based primarily on the ways we have been shaped to understand the world around us. Just as people evaluated Jesus' claim to being Messiah based on how they had been formed to understand what it meant to *be* Messiah, so we inevitably find ourselves evaluating such things as our marriages, our jobs, and our churches on the basis of how we've been formed to think about the purpose of each of these. If I've been formed all of my life, for example, to believe that marriage is primarily a means to personal happiness, then it will make perfectly good sense for me to evaluate my marriage on whether or not it is furthering my happiness. In fact, my daily experience of marriage will likely be inseparable from my ongoing assessment of whether it is indeed furthering my happiness.

Now what does any of this have to do with Christian formation? Quite a lot, actually.

All of us are constantly being formed by the cultures of which we are a part. As noted before, whether we know it or not, or whether we like it or not, formation happens. This means that the question is never simply *whether* we are being formed; we are. Rather, the more important question is always this: *Into what* are we being formed? As Christians who are called to be conformed to the image of Christ, we ought to have a keen interest in the ways our lives and the lives of those around us are being formed. In short, we need to pay attention to the shape of our lives.

As noted above, every culture forms its citizens to see the world and act within it in certain ways that are regarded as "normal" within that culture. This process of formation is obviously complicated, but we can begin to get a bit of a handle on it by paying attention to some of the most important parts of this process. Every culture nourishes a certain way of life, a certain way of looking at and living in the world. This way of life has a number of interlocking elements that include at least the following:

- A certain set of *desires* or *longings*. What do we want out of life? What should we most desire?
- A certain set of *convictions* or *core beliefs* regarding such things as the purpose of life, the way the world works and one's place within it, and the proper means for evaluating success or failure in life.
- A certain set of *dispositions* or *inclinations* to act in certain ways that taken together we call *character*.

Furthermore, every culture goes about nourishing and instilling these desires, convictions and dispositions by a number of means, including the following:

- Telling certain *stories*.

- ◆ Engaging in certain *practices*.
- ◆ Building and sustaining certain *institutions*.

The next six conversations in this study will take up each one of these central aspects of formation. Because these six aspects are closely intertwined, we could reasonably begin with any one of them and then proceed to discuss the others. Thus, the order in which these six elements are taken up should not be viewed as a commentary on their relative importance but merely as an admission that it's difficult to try to talk about six things at once!

As you proceed through this study in the coming weeks and are asked to think hard about and pay attention to matters that often escape our attention, always try to keep in mind the central reason for undertaking this study: as followers of Jesus Christ, we have been called to have our lives formed and animated by the Spirit of Jesus. Yet how shall we discern whether or to what extent that is indeed happening? One possible way to put ourselves in a better position to make such discernments is to explore how human beings come to be formed and animated. Once we get a better handle on how we are being formed and animated in our everyday lives, we may be in a better position to ask more pointed questions about who or what is predominantly influencing the overall shape of our lives.

Questions for Personal Reflection and Group Discussion

1. As you think about your life, what people, events, and experiences do you think have been the most formative for who you are today? It may help you to complete this sentence: "If it hadn't have been for _____, I don't think I'd be who I am today." Take one or two of these major formative influences and reflect carefully on how specifically you came to be formed through them.

Aunt Marie
Beatrice Edgerton

2. Has there been a time in your life when you were intensely aware that you were being formed? If so, what were the circumstances and what contributed to this awareness? If not, do you think this necessarily means that you weren't being formed?

② graduate school
their values were not my values
everybody else was stupid
① relationship with A.E. church

3. As you think about your family members, your friends, your co-workers, and your neighbors, what would you identify as some as the most formative influences on their lives? What basis do you have for thinking so?

Christianity → what's right fr. wrong
their chosen professions - teaching
engineering

4. You'll be encouraged over the next several weeks to think carefully about the ways in which your faith community functions as a community of formation. What do you think are some of the most obvious ways in which your congregation or parish functions as a community of formation? In other words, where are some of the places where you see formation taking place on a regular basis? Where else might it also be taking place in less obvious ways?

caring, lending a hand, giving advice.

Paying Greater Attention

You're going to be talking together a lot about formation in the coming weeks. But you won't simply be *talking* about formation, as important as that is. You'll also be asked to examine carefully your corporate and individual lives to see the ways in which they are being shaped. Such examination is rarely easy and almost always convicting. Therefore, pray that in the coming days God will open your eyes to what you need to see and that God will use your humble and honest attempts to pay attention to the shape of your life in ways that will ultimately lead to God's glory.

Conversation #2: Desires

Revealing desires

Most of us would probably admit that one of the primary animating forces in our lives is *desire*. Indeed, if there's some truth to the old adage that "We are what we eat," then there's also likely some truth to the notion that "We are what we want." This is because who we are and who we become are intimately connected to our past, present and future desires.

What is it that you care most deeply about? What are your deepest desires, dreams, and aspirations? What is the desired future you find yourself striving to live into? Whether we are conscious of it or not, these desires have an enormous impact on the shape and experience of our everyday lives. It takes only a moment's reflection to realize that a particular way of life is shaped not only by a person's past, but also by a particular desired and imagined future. In other words, just as our pasts are never simply past (because that past still shapes and influences our present life), so the future we imagine is never simply future (because much of our present energy is expended seeking to live into that imagined future.)

Now what are these desires and where do they come from? Not surprisingly, not everyone agrees about this. Some believe that we are born with certain basic needs and the desire to meet them. These needs may be physiological (air, food, sleep), psychological (stability, security) or social (to belong and be loved). Other people aren't so sure, arguing that even if we have these basic needs, the particular ways in which we learn to recognize them *as* needs and meet them are just that—learned. Still others have argued that all our desires and longings—whatever they are—are simply pointers to the *one* desire that God created at the center of every person: the desire to be in communion with God. It was this desire that Augustine addressed when he spoke of our restless hearts.

Now it is important to note that Christian teaching is *not* that human desire is evil and therefore to be extinguished. Indeed, according to the Christian faith, our problem as humans is not that our lives are animated by desire, but that our lives are so often driven by the *wrong* desires. As a result, the Christian life is about being formed to desire the right things in the right ways for the right reasons. To repeat: Christians are not those who lack or suppress all desire, but those who (by God's grace) are learning to desire rightly.

So how do we learn to desire rightly?

Our desires and God's desires

Perhaps one place to start is with the frank acknowledgement that what most of us have typically been formed to desire for ourselves and what God desires for us are usually quite different. To paraphrase God's insistence in Isaiah 55:8: "My desires are not your desires, nor my longings your longings." This is not least because we live in a society that forms us to pursue relentlessly our own desires, our own happiness. Interestingly enough, in the United States we even have a name for a particular set of longings and desires that we are all encouraged to pursue: we call it "the American Dream." But followers of Jesus know that life isn't simply about pursuing their own happiness or even the happiness of their children or family members. Indeed, those who seek to follow the way of Jesus know that life is not first of all about doing what we desire, but about doing what God desires. Or even more to the point, followers of Jesus seek to be so transformed that one day their own desires will be aligned with God's desires. Just as Jesus' prayer in the Garden of Gethsemane—"not my will but yours be done"—was characteristic of his entire life, so we seek to be animated by God's desires for us and for God's world. This, after all, is surely part of what we ask in praying the Lord's Prayer:

> Your kingdom come,
> Your will be done,
> On earth as it is in heaven. (Matt. 6:10)

We pray and work for the day when God's desires are as fully enacted in our lives and throughout all of God's creation as they are in that realm we call heaven.

What are God's desires? Obviously, there's no short answer to that. But just as we sometimes use the phrase "the American Dream" as a shorthand for that

> *We pray and work for the day when God's desires are fully enacted.*

vision of a particular future that many devote their entire lives to pursuing (and sustaining), so the gospels speak of the "kingdom of God" or the "reign of God" as that social order toward which God is moving all of creation and to which God's people offer themselves in service.

What desires animate that kingdom? We glimpse part of an answer in Luke 15, where Jesus is faced with the grumbling of the scribes and Pharisees who were offended that Jesus was welcoming and eating with tax collectors and other notorious sinners. In response, Jesus tells three parables (the lost sheep, the lost coin, and the lost sons), each of which in its own way underscores one of the central truths of the gospel: God has an unquenchable desire for *us*, a desire that leads God to pursue us relentlessly and to rejoice when we are found. The shepherd leaves behind the other sheep and goes looking for the one lost sheep; the woman searches diligently for her one lost coin until she finds it; and the father, seeing his returning son in the distance, violates all social propriety and runs rejoicing to embrace him.

Thus, whatever we might say about the desires that Christians have or ought to have, such statements should always be framed by the recognition that just as "we love because God first loved us" (1 Jn. 4:19), so also we desire and pursue God because God first desires and pursues us. And as the apostle Paul declares in Romans, there's no reason to believe that God's desires will be easily thwarted:

> For I am convinced that neither death, nor life, nor angels, nor rulers, nor things present, nor things to come, nor powers, nor height, nor depth, nor anything else in all creation, will be able to separate us from the love of God in Christ Jesus our Lord. (Rom. 8:38-39)

We will have much more to say about the relationship of the church to God's kingdom in the second study in this series: "The Shape of God's Reign." For now it is

> **We desire God because God first desires us.**

enough to begin to pay greater attention to the potential conflict between the desires that our culture teaches us to pursue and the desires that God wishes for us. At the very least, formation entails both paying close attention to the desires that currently animate our daily lives, and being open to cultivating a different set of desires that will be at the center of our lives.

Schooling Our Wants

One helpful way we might summarize all of this is by considering how it is that human desire is "educated"—that is, how our varied wants and longings are not untainted, unformed private wishes but are, instead, expressions of our being schooled over time in particular kinds of formative environments: family life, say, or popular culture or mass media. If, for instance, the advertising industry instructs us in what kind of car we should want or what it is that constitutes the "good life," thoughtful Christians will need to be alert to the ways that such an education of desire is at odds with the call to a different kind of life and a different set of desires. We will need to regularly remind ourselves and each other that life in the body of Christ is its own school of counter-formation for those who seek to have their desires educated differently.

This call to a different life, a life marked by a different set of desires, is expressed clearly in 1 Peter:

Therefore prepare your minds for action; discipline yourselves; set all your hope on the grace that Jesus Christ will bring you when he is revealed. Like obedient children, do not be conformed to the desires that you formerly had in ignorance. Instead, as he who called you is holy, be holy yourselves in all your conduct; for it is written, "You shall be holy, for I am holy." (1 Peter 1:13-16).

Scripture for Further Study

The role of desire in human life is not a peripheral theme of scripture. In addition to the passages listed at the beginning of this study, you are encouraged to examine the following texts to gain a better sense of the many ways in which scripture speaks of desire. Make notes of what you learn about desire from each passage.

Genesis 3:1-7

2 Chronicles 15

Psalm 84

Hosea 6:4-6 (with echoes in Matt. 9:13 and 12:7)

Mark 4:13-20

Romans 13:11-14

Galatians 5:16-17

James 1:12-18

1 Peter 2:11-12

1 John 2:15-17

Questions for Personal Reflection and Group Discussion

1. What do you think are the two or three desires or longings that most definitively shape the course of your daily life? How did these come to play such a central role in your life?

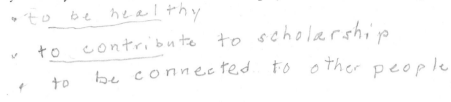

- to be healthy
- to contribute to scholarship
- to be connected to other people

2. If you were to identify one or two desires that you wish had a *greater impact* on the shape of your daily life, what would they be? How do you think your daily life would be different if these desires exerted a greater impact?

- to be closer to God

3. Where in your life do you most feel the tension or conflict of competing desires? In other words, where are the two or three places in your life where your different longings seem to be at odds (if not at war) with each other, resulting in your being pulled in very different (if not opposite) directions?

achieving in scholarship

4. If you were to name the two or three common desires that most give shape to your life as a congregation or parish, what would you name? How do you think these desires came to be shared and to play such a central role in your common life?

helping the poor
worship
intellectual stimulation

5. Are there desires or longings that you wish had a greater shaping impact on your common life as a community of faith? If so, which ones? How do you imagine that your common life would be different if these desires were more central?

greater inclusivity — — e. g. Republicans,
gun-owners, etc.

6. Where in your common life as a faith community do you feel most acutely the tension or conflict of competing desires? How would you name these tensions or conflicts? What are some of the ways in which those tensions manifest themselves?

desire for connections, friendships ⟶
cliquishness — the choir, the people
whose children went to Sunday school
together, who talks with whom
after church.

Paying Greater Attention

1. Try to notice some specific examples of how what you think, do and feel this week are animated by your deepest desires. Jot down a couple of examples here.

I connected

2. Also try to notice some specific examples this week of how what others think, do and feel seem likewise to be animated by what you take to be their deepest desires. Jot down a couple of examples here.

3. Pay attention to the many voices around you this week. What are these voices telling you that you ought to desire? Make a list of some of these here.

A Prayer by A. W. Tozer (from *The Pursuit of God*)

O God, I have tasted Thy goodness, and it has both satisfied me and made me thirsty for more. I am painfully conscious of my need of further grace. I am ashamed of my lack of desire. O God, the Triune God, I want to want Thee; I long to be filled with longing; I thirst to be made more thirsty still. Show me Thy glory, I pray Thee, so that I may know Thee indeed. Begin in mercy a new work of love within me. Say to my soul, "Rise up, my love, my fair one, and come away." Then give me grace to rise and follow Thee up from this misty lowland where I have wandered so long. In Jesus' Name, Amen.

Conversation #3: Convictions

> *O Most High, when I am afraid, I put my trust in you.*
> *In God, whose word I praise, in God I trust;*
> *I am not afraid; what can flesh do to me? (Psalm 56:3-4)*
>
> *Jesus said to them, "But who do you say that I am?"*
> *Simon Peter answered, "You are the Messiah, the Son of the living God."*
> *(Matt. 16:15-16)*
>
> *But if we have died with Christ, we believe that we will also live with him. We know that Christ, being raised from the dead, will never die again; death no longer has dominion over him. The death he died, he died to sin, once for all; but the life he lives, he lives to God. So you also must consider yourselves dead to sin and alive to God in Christ Jesus." (Rom. 6:8-11)*
>
> *We believe in one God, the Father, the Almighty, maker of heaven and earth, of all that is, seen and unseen. We believe in one Lord, Jesus Christ, the only son of God, eternally begotten of the Father, God from God, Light from Light, true God from true God . . . . (Opening words of the Nicene Creed, 4th century)*

"This I Believe"

In the early 1950s, celebrated journalist Edward R. Murrow produced and hosted a popular radio program entitled, "This I Believe." The purpose of the program was to allow citizens from all walks of life an opportunity to articulate the fundamental convictions or core beliefs that guided their everyday lives. In the spring of 2005 a new series of "This I Believe" essays were broadcast on public radio stations across the United States. Although neither program presumed to tell listeners what they should believe, both programs rightly assumed that if we are to understand what animates the lives of our neighbors then we will need to understand their fundamental beliefs or convictions.

Convictions are those deeply held beliefs that shape and inform our everyday experience of the world. How do convictions do this? In short, because the convictions we have about the world suggest both how we ought to live in that believed-in world *and* how to evaluate our current life within it. To get a feel for how this works, ask yourself the following set of questions:

- Do you believe that human life has a purpose? If so, what would you say it is?

- What does it mean to live a good life? In other words, what kinds of things are necessary for human well-being and flourishing? What does a person fundamentally "need" to live well?

- Do you believe that human beings have a basic nature? If so, how would you characterize it?

- Do you believe that people can change?

- Do you think people generally get what they deserve, or do you tend to think that life is basically unfair?

- Who or what is worthy of your complete trust?

Although the answers to none of these questions are simple or straightforward, we all likely have rather well-defined convictions about each one. But where did these deeply-held beliefs come from? Again, none of us came out of the womb believing what we do about these and countless other matters. None of us likely took a class that gave us the answers to any of these questions. Indeed, odds are that most of us give very little direct attention to any of these matters on a regular basis.

Yet it would be a huge mistake to assume that such fundamental convictions—and others like them—don't affect the shape and direction of our everyday lives.

The strength of our convictions

Every culture encourages us to believe some things rather than others about these and other fundamental questions. Such convictions are central to our identity because they represent part of the reservoir we draw from to live our daily lives. For example, do you believe that all or most poor people are lazy, and are therefore largely responsible for their own plight? If so, then you will have certain ideas about what it means to help them. Do you believe that most strangers will hurt you if given the opportunity? If so, this conviction will shape your understanding of what it means to engage in the biblical practice of hospitality. Do you believe that sometimes war and violence are the only possible responses to evil in the

> *Convictions are those deeply held beliefs that shape and inform our everyday experience of the world.*

world? If so, this will likely shape the way you hear Jesus' call to love our enemies and his call to pray for those who persecute us. In short, our convictions go a long way toward shaping our imaginations regarding the kind of world we live in and what it means to live and act in that world. Thus the beliefs we hold are not mere mental operations or private opinions; our convictions exert a profound influence on how we "see" the world around us and how we behave in it.

And since all of us act in the world that our convictions help us to see (a world is inherently unjust, for instance), asking hard questions about such beliefs (and where they come from) is crucial to those who desire to be conformed to the image of Christ.

In future conversations we will take up the issue more directly of *how* these convictions are formed within us; for now, our aim is simply to become more aware of the central role that convictions play in our experience and assessment of everyday life. One way to deepen this awareness is to pay attention to the convictions that inform our lives and the lives of those around us, since the ways people think, feel and act are nearly always closely related to their deepest convictions. For example, imagine that you have an acquaintance named Tom who believes that human life is basically a "race to the top." For Tom, the whole point of human existence is to excel in one's chosen field and climb as high and as quickly as possible up that field's ladder of success. Not surprisingly, this fundamental conviction will inevitably guide many of Tom's decisions and actions in (and beyond) the workplace. It's likely, for instance, that Tom will view fellow co-workers primarily as competitors for scarce resources such as promotions, raises and titles. As a result, Tom will be less inclined to work cooperatively with others, since aiding another's advancement might impede his own. Tom might also be inclined to view home life primarily as a personal support system that enables and facilitates his race to the top. To the extent that it functions well in this respect, Tom may feel good about his home life. Should his family, however, unduly complicate or hamper his progress, he may find himself frustrated and dissatisfied with family life.

It's also likely that Tom will find himself evaluating other arenas of his life in similar ways. He may, for example, come to evaluate his experience of the church largely on the basis of how well it supports his chosen life goals. If it facilitates those goals, or perhaps even helps him cope with the fallout from the pursuit of those goals, then he may find himself evaluating his church experience positively. If, however, the church ever begins to question the fundamental appropriateness of those life goals, Tom may find himself irritated by what he perceives as the church's "meddling" in his personal affairs.

Of course it's not simply Tom's experience of work, home or church life that come to be evaluated in terms of his guiding conviction about the point or

> *The ways people think, feel and act are nearly always closely related to their deepest convictions.*

purpose of life. Tom's overall sense of how a particular day or week went, or even how his life in general is going, will inevitably be tied to his sense of how much progress he is making up the ladder.

The point of this simple example is to help us see how a single guiding conviction can have an enormous impact on the shape and experience of one's life. The way we think, the way we act, the way we feel—all usually have direct ties to the deep convictions we hold. Of course, the reality of our everyday lives is much more complicated than the above example, not least because our lives are usually guided by a number of different (and sometimes competing or conflicting) convictions.

Yet the example can nevertheless encourage us to examine our core beliefs, the fundamental convictions that guide our everyday decisions. If you were asked, for example, to sit down right now and write an essay for the "This I Believe" series that would articulate your core convictions and thereby "make sense" of the shape of your current life, what would you write? What, in other words, would someone need to know about your deepest convictions in order to make sense of the way you live your life? Or perhaps even more to the point, what might others identify as your deepest convictions by looking at the shape of your current life?

A matter of trust

If you were to write such an essay, it's very likely that one of the primary matters you would address is where you place your trust, for trust is one of the most fundamental orienting factors in human life. Although we're not always aware of it consciously, we all find ourselves placing our trust in something or someone all the time, and this posture of trust goes a long way toward defining the shape our lives. To put this differently: the shape of our lives is influenced not only by what we believe *about* the world, but also by what or who we believe *in*. It's one thing, for example, to believe (intellectually) that your co-worker is trustworthy; it's another to believe *in* that co-worker in the sense of placing your trust in her.

It may be worth noting at this point that the biblical notion of faith involves not simply believing

> *The shape of our lives is influenced not only by what we believe <u>about</u> the world, but also by what or who we believe in.*

that something is the case, but also believing *in* something or someone. As the author of the book of James suggests, even the demons are orthodox (in the sense of holding right beliefs), for even they believe that God is one (2:19). So presumably the difference between the demons and those who follow Jesus is not primarily a matter of what they believe *about* God; rather, the difference is a matter of trust *in* God. The demons refuse to place their trust in God and the ways of God, while followers of Jesus are called to do precisely that.

Our convictions about who or what is worthy of our trust go a long way toward defining the shape of our lives. In his letter to the Romans, the apostle Paul explained the centrality of faith and trust to the Christian life by appealing to the example of our father in the faith, Abraham:

> Hoping against hope, he believed that he would become "the father of many nations," according to what was said, "So numerous shall your descendents be." He did not weaken in faith when he considered his own body, which was already as good as dead (for he was about a hundred years old), or when he considered the barrenness of Sarah's womb. No distrust made him waver concerning the promise of God, but he grew strong in his faith as he gave glory to God, being fully convinced that God was able to do what he had promised. (Rom. 4:18-21)

Abraham trusted God because he was convinced that God was able to do what God had promised. Of course, like all of us, Abraham was not as steadfast as the God who called him, and so Abraham sometimes trusted his own ways more than the ways of God. (See Genesis 16 for one obvious example.) Nevertheless, we—like Abraham—are called to place our trust in God and the ways of God. Indeed, such trust, such faith, is to be the fundamental posture of entire lives.

But is it? If we are honest with ourselves about our everyday lives, in what or whom do we actually place our trust? More than likely, over the course of a day or week, most of us place (or are encouraged to place) varying degrees of trust in quite a number of different things: our family members; our neighbors and co-workers; strangers in the car next to us speeding down the highway; the laws of the land and our system of government; our police and military forces; our physical senses; the general orderliness of the universe; our reason and education; our experience and "instincts"; and our own abilities and hard work—just to name a few. That's a lot of trust. We could, of course, devote a lot of time arguing whether it's appropriate to place our trust in any of these things, and scripture would have some important things to say to us about this. Yet most of us probably know—at least intellectually—that we are called to place our ultimate trust in the God of Jesus Christ. So here's the real question: in light of all these things that we routinely place our trust in, what would it mean—and just as importantly, what might it *look like*—for us to say, with the psalmist, that we place our trust in God?

The way that leads to life

Certainly no brief study can do justice to what it means to place our trust fully in God. Yet perhaps a couple of central issues can be raised in ways that will place this crucial matter at the center of the church's agenda once again and offer thoughtful Christians plenty to think about and discuss together.

Most of us would acknowledge that trusting God means placing our very lives in God's hands. Yet what does that look like in daily life? At a minimum, it requires us to live our lives trusting that there is more to life than we can see with our human eyes. It requires us to trust that in the person of Jesus we really do come face to face with God and the ways of God. It requires us to trust that the ways of God really do lead to life. This fundamental posture of trust is rooted in one of the most central convictions of the church: that in Jesus Christ we see most clearly who God is. But the church has *also* always insisted that in Jesus Christ we also see most clearly who *we* are called to be, for in Christ we see what it means to be fully human. In Jesus Christ, therefore, we

> **In Jesus Christ we see most clearly who God is and who we are called to be.**

receive not only the most complete image available of what God is like, but also the most complete image available of what it means to be fully human. God's call to be conformed to the image of Christ, therefore, is a call to life, a call to live life as it was created to be lived.

But walking in the way of Jesus—a way that is grounded in mercy, compassion and forgiveness—will require us to trust in the ways of God, because the wide and well-worn ways of the world lead in an entirely different direction. The world forms us to believe that the way of Jesus is impractical, utopian, and unrealistic. In contrast, followers of Jesus live their lives based on the conviction that the way of Jesus is not simply God's way of dealing with us, but also the way God desires us to deal with others. In short, as Christians we are called to trust fully that human life is never more beautiful than when it is lived in conformity to the way of Jesus. Such a life is one that is not only marked by integrity and wholeness, but one which is itself dedicated to being an *agent* of healing and wholeness in the world—a vessel through which the love and mercy of God freely flows.

There are, of course, many, many obstacles to living such a life. We live in a culture that is increasingly animated less by trust than by its opposite: fear. As inhabitants of this culture we find ourselves torn almost daily between the call to trust God and God's ways and the temptation to be driven by our own fears, real and imagined. Throughout our lifetimes, all of us face fears of different kinds: of failure, of rejection, of injury and illness, and ultimately, of death itself. But a life lived in the grip of fear has little hope of being a beautiful life. The good news of the gospel, however, is that in Jesus Christ we are freed from the stranglehold that fear—including the fear of death—has on our lives. In Jesus Christ we are freed to live an abundant life, a life grounded in a fundamental trust of God and the ways of God. For as Paul poignantly asked his brothers and sisters in Rome, "if God is for us, who can be against us?" (Rom 8:31)

One of the fundamental convictions of the Christian faith is that the God revealed in Jesus Christ is worthy of our ultimate trust and allegiance. Are followers of Jesus—by virtue of being followers of Jesus—called to hold other fundamental convictions about the world and their place within it? If so, what are these fundamental "Christian" convictions and in what ways are they similar to and different from the convictions that other people hold? And how exactly are Christians in their everyday lives to live out these convictions?

These are all important questions; indeed, the point of this study is to encourage conversations that might help us begin formulating thoughtful responses to such crucial matters. Are there easy answers to these questions? Probably not. But there's a good chance that in discussing them seriously with one another we might begin to see more clearly both the shape of our current lives and the shape of the life to which God has called us.

Food for Thought

In a recent "This I Believe" radio essay, journalist Sara Miles spoke of how her idea of "belief" changed when she—an avowed skeptic—received communion for the first time. In her own words:

I came to believe that God is revealed not only in bread and wine during church services, but whenever we share food with others — particularly strangers. I came to believe that the fruits of creation are for everyone, without exception — not something to be doled out to insiders or the "deserving."

So, over the objections of some of my fellow parishioners, I started a food pantry right in the church sanctuary, giving away literally tons of oranges and potatoes and Cheerios around the very same altar where I'd eaten the body of Christ. We gave food to anyone who showed up. I met thieves, child abusers, millionaires, day laborers, politicians, schizophrenics, gangsters, bishops — all blown into my life through the restless power of a call to feed people.

At the pantry, serving over 500 strangers a week, I confronted the same issues that had kept me from religion in the first place. Like church, the food pantry asked me to leave certainty behind, tangled me up with people I didn't particularly want to know and scared me with its demand for more faith than I was ready to give.

Because my new vocation didn't turn out to be as simple as going to church on Sundays and declaring myself "saved." I had to trudge in the rain through housing projects, sit on the curb wiping the runny nose of a psychotic man, take the firing pin out of a battered woman's Magnum and then stick the gun in a cookie tin in the trunk of my car. I had to struggle with my atheist family, my doubting friends, and the prejudices and traditions of my newfound church.

But I learned that hunger can lead to more life — that by sharing real food, I'd find communion with the most unlikely people; that by eating a piece of bread, I'd experience myself as part of one body. This I believe: that by opening ourselves to strangers, we will taste God.

Source: www.npr.org

Questions for Personal Reflection and Group Discussion

1. Take the time to identify two or three fundamental convictions or core beliefs that clearly shape the course of your daily life. (If you need help getting started, you may want to refer back to the list at the beginning of this conversation to remind yourself of what some of these might be.) In what specific ways do these convictions influence the shape of your life? How did these come to play such a central role in your life?

(2) in the end, working hard and persistence will get you somewhere. e.g. going to church writing this paper after 30 yrs

(1) I'm not as good as other people, but I sometimes act like I am.

2. If you were to name one or two convictions that you wish had a *greater impact* on the shape of your daily life, what would they be? How do you imagine that your life would be different if they *did* have a greater shaping influence? How do you account for the relative lack of influence that these convictions have on the shape of your life currently?

That I am as a that I do have something to give good as other people.

3. As you reflect on your community of faith, who comes to mind when you think of people whose everyday lives are marked by a fundamental posture of trust in God and the ways of God? What is it about the shape of these people's lives that suggests that they trust God deeply? Where in your own life do you trust God? Where do you sense a lack of trust in God?

Karen — her decision to leave the insurance industry

Frances May

4. If you were to name the two or three shared convictions or core beliefs that most give shape to your life as a congregation or parish, what would you name? How did these convictions come to be shared and have such a central role? Do you think most people in your congregation or parish would identify the same convictions? Why or why not?

• as a congregation we need to give to the community

• everyone can have a role in church life

5. Are there particular convictions that you wish had a greater shaping impact on your common life as a community of faith? If so, which ones? How do you imagine that your common life would be different if these convictions were more central?

Paying Greater Attention

1. Try to notice some specific examples this week of how what you think, do and feel are informed by un-named but very real and present convictions that you hold. Jot down a couple of examples here.

trust in an editor whom I've never met —partly inspired by
that people a therapist; partly inspired by the
are kind-hearted Notre Dame hallmark.

2. Also try to notice some specific examples this week of how what others think, do and feel seem likewise to be informed by un-named but very real and present convictions that they hold. Jot down a couple of examples here.

supports
Linda Westman's excitement about my plan to go to Cape May
genuine love for others

Identity
Thomas Merton

If you want to identify me,
ask me not where I live,
or what I like to eat, or
how I comb my hair;
but ask me what I am living for,
in detail, and ask me
what I think is keeping me
from living fully for
the thing I want to live for.

Source: "My Argument with the Gestapo," by Thomas Merton.

Conversation #4: Character

The LORD is merciful and gracious, slow to anger and abounding in steadfast love. He will not always accuse, nor will he keep his anger forever. He does not deal with us according to our sins, nor repay us according to our iniquities. For as the heavens are high above the earth, so great is his steadfast love toward those who fear him; as far as the east is from the west, so far he removes our transgressions from us. As a father has compassion for his children, so the LORD has compassion for those who fear him. (Ps. 103:8-13)

As God's chosen ones, holy and beloved, clothe yourselves with compassion, kindness, humility, meekness, and patience. Bear with one another and, if anyone has a complaint against another, forgive each other; just as the Lord has forgiven you, so you also must forgive. Above all, clothe yourselves with love, which binds everything together in perfect harmony. And let the peace of Christ rule in your hearts, to which indeed you were called in the one body. And be thankful. (Colossians 3:12-15)

You are the salt of the earth; but if salt has lost its taste, how can its saltiness be restored? It is no longer good for anything, but is thrown out and trampled under foot. You are the light of the world. A city built on a hill cannot be hid. No one after lighting a lamp puts it under the bushel basket, but on the lampstand, and it gives light to all in the house. In the same way, let your light shine before others, so that they may see your good works and give glory to your Father in heaven. (Matt. 5:13-16)

The character of our lives

Every culture forms its inhabitants to be inclined to act in certain ways. How are you inclined to act, for example, if you find yourself in a car sitting at a stoplight and the only car in front of you hasn't moved an inch five seconds after the light has turned green? How are you disposed to respond when you are at a party and someone insults you or cuts you down? Or how are you likely to respond when you get word that one of your personal enemies—someone who has gone out of his or her way to make your life miserable—suddenly has a bit of misfortune themselves?

To say that all of us have been formed in ways that incline us toward certain responses in such situations is not to excuse our responses, whatever they might be. Rather, it is to acknowledge that the dynamics of human behavior are often more complicated than they first appear. Up to this point we have noted that people are animated both by certain *desires* and by certain *convictions* they hold about the world and their place within it. We now turn to look briefly at another dimension of our "shape," an aspect that is both formed by those around us and serves as another animating force in our lives. This dimension we call *character*.

We use the language of character to point to something important (yet elusive) about the dynamics of human behavior: the fact that human behavior is neither completely predictable nor completely random. Rather, over time the lives of people show certain patterns and take on a certain shape such that we feel justified in making certain judgments about the kind of people they are. The distinctive shape of a human life made visible through certain patterns of behavior is what we mean by "character." We see our neighbor battle with cancer over many months with an indomitable spirit and we feel justified in calling her "courageous" and "brave." We work for years for an employer who consistently looks out for the well-being of all of his employees and we feel justified in saying that he is "just" and "fair." Over the years we watch a mother care for her disabled little boy, striving to help him cope with the basics of life, and we feel justified in calling her "patient" and "steadfast."

Does this mean that our neighbor has never acted cowardly, or that our employer has never acted unjustly, or that this mother has never lost her patience with her little boy? Of course not. Rather, it means that we have seen enough of this person's life to feel confident about the ways in which they are typically inclined or disposed to act.

> *The distinctive shape of a human life made visible through certain patterns of behavior is what we mean by "character."*

Can we ever predict for sure how they or anyone else will act in a particular situation? No, but we still think it possible to name certain commendable patterns that we see in people's lives, patterns that we call by such names as "courage," "justice," and "patience." These qualities, which we often refer to as "virtues," allow us not so much to predict another person's behavior as they enable us to point to behavior we think worthy of imitation.

In short, over time each of us is formed in such a way as to be inclined or disposed to act in certain ways rather than others. When these inclinations and dispositions result in patterns of behavior that are commendable and worthy of imitation we name them as virtues; when they result in patterns of behavior to be avoided we name them as vices. The distinctive shape of a life resulting from all of this taken together is what we mean by character.

But how do we determine the kinds of behavior worth imitating? How do we determine which virtues are to be nurtured and which vices avoided? To answer that question, we need to explore a bit further the notion of "virtue."

The excellence of Christ

For many of us, virtue language has been all but ruined, conjuring up images of prudes and other killjoys whom we imagine promoting some rigid set of rules. If this is what it means to be "virtuous," we think, then many of us want nothing to do with it. But the concept of virtue is much broader (and much more interesting!) than this. In fact, whether we ever use the word or not, the concept of virtue is woven deeply into the fabric of any society or culture.

What is a virtue? At its most basic level, a virtue is simply a form of excellence. For example, the virtues of a championship race horse are its strength, speed and stamina, while one of the virtues of a fine watch is its accuracy in keeping time. Similarly, we are frequently told that ketchup ought to be thick and computers ought to be user-friendly. These examples raise two important issues. First, the "virtue" or "excellence" of something is always tied directly to what we take to be the *purpose* of that thing. In other words, if you're convinced that the purpose of a watch is to keep accurate time, then you'll have a ready basis on which to make judgments about whether this or that watch displays this excellence or virtue. And second, although each of the four examples listed above seems fairly straightforward, part of what makes them appear so is that there are relatively widespread agreements about the purposes of race horses, watches, ketchups and computers.

Thus, even though nearly everything around us can (and is) evaluated according to some standard of excellence (or virtue), the more people disagree about the purpose of something, the more that people will likely disagree about what will count for excellence. What are the virtues of a good restaurant? That will depend upon your convictions regarding the primary purposes of restaurants. What makes a good elementary school? That will depend upon what you think schools are for. In a similar way, when people make judgments about the "virtues" of a particular congregation or parish, they are revealing—whether they recognize it or not—their convictions about what they think the purpose of the church is. Not surprisingly, if people disagree about the fundamental purposes of restaurants, schools or churches they will also likely disagree about what makes a "good" or "excellent" one.

As you might imagine, matters are no less complicated when we turn to human beings. What virtues or excellences should humans embody? How should human beings be disposed to act in certain situations? To answer these questions is already to reveal one's convictions about the fundamental purposes of human life. In short, any list of virtues or human excellences (and vices) reveals what people believe the shape of life ought (or ought not) to look like. Thus, when public schools seek through character education programs to instill in students certain "civic virtues" (such as civility, open-mindedness and respect for authority), they reveal something about the kind of people they believe are necessary for a democratic society to function well. In a similar way, employers who seek to instill in their employees "workplace virtues" such as reliability, loyalty and efficiency do so because people with such virtues will help that enterprise be successful.

> **The excellence that Christians are called to live out is the excellence they see revealed in Jesus Christ.**

To ask about the virtues or the patterns of behavior that ought to be at the heart of the Christian life is likewise to inquire about the desired shape of human life. Here, however, the goal is not primarily a responsible citizen or a productive employee, but a child of God conformed to the image of Jesus Christ. In other words, the virtue or excellence that Christians are called to live out is the excellence they see revealed in the one who lived human life as it was intended to be lived—Jesus Christ. Thus, the church is called to be a community of compassion as a witness to the compassionate God revealed first to Israel and then most perfectly in and through Jesus Christ. Our character, in short, ought to reflect something of the character of God.

Of course, as Christians we do not believe that we can live such lives of virtue or excellence apart from God's grace and the working of God's Spirit. Nevertheless, we do believe that God can transform the shape of our lives and the patterns of our behavior to bring them more into conformity to the pattern we see in Jesus Christ. After all, if we claim that we are followers of Jesus, and if we insist that the Spirit of Christ is working in and through us, shouldn't we expect that over time some transformation would take place? The apostle Paul was convinced that the Spirit is transforming us into the image of Christ:

> And all of us, with unveiled faces, seeing the glory of the Lord as though reflected in a mirror, are being transformed into the same image from one degree of glory to another; for this comes from the Lord, the Spirit. (2 Cor. 3:18)

Paul also was very clear that this transformation was not merely an invisible transformation that left everything as it was; rather, this transformation involved bearing real behavioral fruit, fruit that was the natural outcome of the Spirit's work in our lives:

> The fruit of the Spirit is love, joy, peace, patience, kindness, generosity, faithfulness, gentleness, and self-control. (Gal 5:22-23)

So learning to pay attention to the fruit (the virtues or vices) being nurtured in our lives is not for the purpose of encouraging pride (or despair) but so that we might cultivate the kind of alert, honest reckoning necessary for the life of discipleship. How will we know if the Spirit is bearing good fruit in our lives if we're afraid to look and see what fruit is actually growing there? Moreover, the church also

> *The church's life together is a potentially eloquent witness to the power of God's Spirit to transform the shape of human life.*

pays attention to the character of its life together because that life is a potentially eloquent witness to the power of God's Spirit to transform the shape of human life. As Jesus suggests in the passage from the Sermon on the Mount quoted above, we are called to be "salt" and "light" not for our own sake, but for the sake of those around us, so that it in seeing our good works others may give glory to God.

This is why Paul could boldly encourage others to "be imitators of me, as I am of Christ" (1 Cor. 11:1). Paul did not believe that the Christian life consisted only in believing certain things about Jesus Christ, but also in the willingness to be transformed by God's grace into the people we were created to be. But doing so required that Paul's listeners be willing to set their minds on certain things and to keep on *doing* certain things as well. May we take his words of admonition to heart as well:

> Finally, beloved, whatever is true, whatever is honorable, whatever is just, whatever is pure, whatever is pleasing, whatever is commendable, if there is any excellence and if there is anything worthy of praise, think about these things. Keep on doing the things that you have learned and received and heard and seen in me, and the God of peace will be with you. (Philippians 4:8-9)

A Study in Character

In his book, *War is a Force that Gives us Meaning,* journalist Chris Hedges tells the story of meeting the Soraks, a Bosnian Serb couple in a largely Muslim enclave of Goražde. The couple had been indifferent to the nationalist propaganda of the Bosnian Serb leadership. But when the Serbs started to bomb their town, the Muslim leadership in the community became hostile to them, and eventually the Soraks lost their two sons to Muslim forces. One of their sons was a few months shy of becoming a father. In the city under siege, conditions got worse and worse, and in the midst of this, Rosa Sorak's widowed daughter-in-law gave birth to a baby girl. With the food shortages, the elderly and infants were dying in droves, and after a short time, the baby, given only tea to drink, began to fade. Meanwhile, on the eastern edge of Goražde, Fadil Fejzić, an illiterate Muslim farmer, kept his cow, milking her by night so as to avoid Serbian snipers. On the fifth day of the baby having only tea, just before dawn, Fejzić appeared at the door with a half a litre of milk for the baby. He refused money. He came back with milk every day for 442 days, until the daughter-in-law and granddaughter left for Serbia. During this time he never said anything. Other families in the street started to insult him, telling him to give his milk to Muslims and let the *četnik* (the pejorative term for Serbs) die. But he did not relent.

Later the Soraks moved, and lost touch with Fejzić. But Hedges went and sought him out. The cow had been slaughtered for meat before the end of the siege, and Fejzić had fallen on hard times. But, as Hedges says, "When I told him I had seen the Soraks, his eyes brightened. 'And the baby?' he asked. 'How is she?'"

Retold by James Alison, *Undergoing God: Dispatches from the Scene of a Break-In* (Continuum, 2006)

In this moving story we see something of how character is lived. The farmer had been formed over time in such a way that generosity and compassion were central to his identity—to his way of being and living in the world, so that even in the face of danger and persecution, he could do no other than to act generously and compassionately.

Scripture for Further Study

Virtues (and vices) are about settled dispositions and habitual patterns of behavior. Although scripture doesn't commonly use the terminology of "virtue" or "character" to identify these patterns, scripture does clearly teach that the lives of the people of God should reflect patterns of behavior brought alive by the Spirit of God.

In addition to the passages mentioned above, reflect on the following passages of scripture, paying particular attention to: 1) the importance of not only *knowing* but *doing* what God desires; 2) the radical difference between our former lives and our lives in Christ; and 3) the importance of imitation and the setting of examples for others to follow. Feel free to jot down additional biblical references that also echo these themes.

Matthew 7:24-27

Matthew 21:28-32

Mark 3:31-35

Luke 11:27-28

John 15:1-11

2 Corinthians 5:16-17

Ephesians 5:1-20

Philippians 3:12-21

Colossians 3:1-3

1 Thessalonians 1:2-10

Titus 3:1-7

Hebrews 13:1-7

James 1:22-25

3 John 1:11

Questions for Personal Reflection and Group Discussion

1. As noted above, every list of virtues is rooted in certain convictions concerning what counts for a good life. Make a list of what you believe are the most important human virtues. Once you have done so, go back over your list and try to discern what your list reveals about your convictions regarding human life and flourishing.

kindness   charity
tolerance
Faithfulness (in a serious relationship)
Fairness
honesty
intelligent but humble (humility)

2. Next, make a list of those virtues that you see most often commended by the wider society (mass media, advertising, popular culture, etc). What does this list reveal about what human life is presumably about?

competitiveness, drive
smart, quick
amoral
physically handsome, beautiful
greedy

3. What do you think are the two or three virtues that are most regularly displayed in your own daily life? Take one of these virtues and reflect on how you came to have this virtue formed within you.

kindness — mother, father, aunt

4. If you were to identify one or two virtues that you wish you displayed more regularly in your daily life, what would they be? Are you able to name any concrete obstacles to the nurturing of these virtues?

tolerance — the street people
people with political views with which I don't agree.

5. If you were to name the two or three virtues that are most regularly displayed in and through your life together as a congregation or parish, what would they be? How do you think these virtues came to be formed in your common life?

Charity
intelligence but humility

6. Are there virtues that you wish were more regularly displayed in your common life as a community of faith? If so, which ones? How do you imagine that your common life would be different if these virtues were more intentionally cultivated?

inclusiveness (tolerance)
alliance with St. Thomas

Paying Greater Attention

This week try to notice some specific examples of virtues that are commended by the wider society. As you hear the news, watch movies, read a book, listen to music, etc., notice the dispositions and patterns of behavior that are praised and commended. Pay particular attention to the ways they are commended and what assumptions about human life go largely unspoken.

Conversation #5: Stories

> *In the beginning, God created the heavens and the earth. The earth was a formless void and darkness covered the face of the deep, while the Spirit of God swept over the face of the waters. Then God said, "Let there be light"; and there was light. And God saw that the light was good. . . . Then God said, "Let us make humankind in our image, according to our likeness; and let them have dominion over the fish of the sea, and over the birds of the air, and over the cattle, and over all the wild animals of the earth, and over every creeping thing that creeps upon the earth." So God created humankind in his image, in the image of God he created them; male and female he created them. (Genesis 1:1-4, 26-27)*
>
> *God also spoke to Moses and said to him: "I am the LORD. I appeared to Abraham, Isaac, and Jacob as God Almighty, but by my name 'The LORD' I did not make myself known to them. I also established my covenant with them, to give them the land of Canaan, the land in which they resided as aliens. I have also heard the groaning of the Israelites whom the Egyptians are holding as slaves, and I have remembered my covenant. Say therefore to the Israelites, 'I am the LORD, and I will free you from the burdens of the Egyptians and deliver you from slavery to them. I will redeem you with an outstretched arm and with mighty acts of judgment. I will take you as my people, and I will be your God. You shall know that I am the Lord your God, who has freed you from the burdens of the Egyptians. I will bring you into the land that I swore to give to Abraham, Isaac, and Jacob; I will give it to you for a possession. I am the LORD.'" (Exodus 6:2-8)*
>
> *When they came to the place that is called The Skull, they crucified Jesus there with the criminals, one on his right and one on his left. Then Jesus said, "Father, forgive them; for they do not know what they are doing." And they cast lots to divide his clothing. And the people stood by, watching; but the leaders scoffed at him, saying, "He saved others; let him save himself if he is the Messiah of God, his chosen one!" (Luke 23:33-35)*
>
> *But on the first day of the week, at early dawn, they came to the tomb, taking the spices that they had prepared. They found the stone rolled away from the tomb, but when they went in, they did not find the body. While they were perplexed about this, suddenly two men in dazzling clothes stood beside them. The women were terrified and bowed their faces to the ground, but the men said to them, "Why do you look for the living among the dead? He is not here, but has risen." (Luke 24:1-5)*

Up to this point we have focused on the *what* of formation, that is, on *what* is being formed. In doing so, we have concentrated primarily on the ways in which our desires, convictions and dispositions are continually being formed.

As we have tried to underscore in the first four conversations, attending to the formation of our desires, convictions, and dispositions is important because these have an enormous influence on the ways we experience and evaluate our everyday lives. In short, the shape of our everyday lives is inseparable from the longings we have, the convictions we hold, and the character we embody. But the shape of our everyday lives is also inseparable from the stories we tell, the practices we engage in, and the institutions which structure and support all the rest. Thus, our next three conversations will shift our focus to these three additional aspects of formation—stories, practices, and institutions—as a way of exploring the *how* of formation.

The centrality of stories

Stories are an incredibly important part of human life. We are, as some have noted, "story-shaped" creatures. Whether we recognize it consciously or not, we are constantly seeking to make sense of our lives and the lives of those around us on the basis of certain stories. For example, if you were given an hour or two to introduce yourself to a group of strangers, you would most likely not offer them a list of disconnected facts about yourself (date of birth, social security number, home address, etc.); rather, you would offer them some version of your "life story." In that story you would no doubt recount for them certain pivotal events, significant relationships and key experiences that you have come to believe offer insight into how you came to be where and who you are. Indeed, we often use phrases like "chapters of our lives," "turning the page," "an open book" or "closing the book" to describe elements of our life story.

Yet we understand ourselves not simply through the personal stories we tell about our own lives, but perhaps even more definitively through the larger, more comprehensive narratives that often frame our personal stories. Jews, for example, have for millennia understood their identity as inseparable from the story of God's covenant with Abraham and of God's action in delivering Abraham's descendents from Egyptian bondage. Indeed, so closely is this God—'the LORD' (in Hebrew, YHWH; Ex. 3:14)—bound to this people that this God is repeatedly identified not as some remote, generic deity, but precisely as "the LORD your God, who brought you out of the land of Egypt" (Ex. 20:2; Lev. 19:36; Num. 15:41; Deut.

5:6). This God, this event, and this people are bound together in ways that can only be understood by retelling and reliving this story. A significant part of what it means to be a Jew, therefore, is to come to understand oneself in terms of this larger, encompassing narrative.

> **We are constantly seeking to make sense of our lives and the lives of those around us on the basis of certain stories.**

Christians likewise come to understand who they are and who they are called to be in light of the story of "God with us" narrated in scripture and retold in and through the life of the church over the centuries. Like Jews, Christians understand themselves as creatures made in the image of God (Gen. 1:26-27), creatures who have been given the responsibility of being faithful stewards of God's good creation. And just as Jews insist that who they are is inseparable from God's promises to their ancestors and God's action in liberating them from Egyptian bondage, so Christians insist that their own identity is inseparable from this same God's action in and through the life, death and resurrection of Jesus of Nazareth and the ongoing work of God's Spirit.

Such claims may seem strange to those of us who are not accustomed to thinking of ourselves (consciously, at least) in terms of such large encompassing stories. Yet it may be that stories play a much larger role in the shape of our lives than we normally think. To begin to understand this, we may need to step back and look more closely at the ways we use stories all the time to make sense of our world and our place in it.

The character of stories

Stories are crucial to human life because we are constantly evaluating ourselves and those around us on the basis of certain stories we tell. Stories are a crucial aspect of our experience of human life not least because actions do not interpret themselves. That is, our actions—and the actions of others—only "make sense" by being placed in some narrative framework or story. All of us have experienced this whenever we have found ourselves misunderstood because the story other people were using to interpret our actions was very different from the story we were telling ourselves about those same actions.

Imagine, for example, that Sue has been coming home late from work every night for a couple of weeks. When her husband, Bob, asks her to try to be home for dinner the next evening, Sue promises to be on time. The next evening, however, Sue walks in the door an hour late. How are we to understand her actions? Clearly, "being an hour-later-than-promised for dinner" neither explains her actions nor gives us (or Bob) enough context to interpret or evaluate her tardiness. Like Bob, we would ask Sue to explain why she was late, at which point Sue would tell a story about what happened. We can, of course, imagine any number of possible stories that Sue might tell, and the point, of course, is that how we evaluate Sue's tardiness will be bound up with the story she tells (and whether or not we believe her).

Presuming for the moment that we have every reason to believe that Sue is telling the truth, notice how our evaluation of Sue changes depending on which of the following two stories she tells:

> *Our actions, or the actions of others, only "make sense" by being placed in some narrative framework or story.*

- ◆ "I'm sorry, Bob, for being late again. I guess that I just got so caught up in the project that I was working on that I totally lost track of time."

- ◆ "I'm sorry, Bob, for being late again. I really tried to be here on time; really, I did. In fact, I wanted to keep my promise so badly that I actually left work 30 minutes early in order to be sure I was on time for dinner. But on the way home I got stuck in a traffic jam caused by a horrible accident and so I didn't have any choice but to just sit there and wait. I tried to phone you to let you know that I'd likely be late, but the line was busy. I hope you'll understand."

This example returns us to the issue of character raised last time. The judgments we make about character are always connected to stories we tell (or are told) that narrate certain patterns of action. In other words, whatever judgments we make about Sue's character will be intimately tied to the ways we narrate (and therefore interpret) her actions. Or said differently, we rarely come to understand a particular virtue (such as faithfulness) by having someone give us a dictionary definition of it; rather, we come to understand such virtues by seeing them displayed and narrated in the lives of those around us.

A similar point could be made about the character of God as revealed in scripture. We come to understand the steadfastness of God as we read of ancient Israel's repeated rebelliousness and God's willingness to take them back. We come to understand something of the breadth of God's mercy as we read the story of Jonah and his mission to Israel's sworn enemies, the Ninevites. And we come to understand something of the depth of God's love as we follow Jesus on his way to the cross. In the same way, the gospels offer us not a list of abstract qualities that Jesus possessed, but stories about his interactions with Pharisees and prostitutes, children and tax collectors. And we know from the gospel accounts that Jesus' actions were open (like ours) to more than one interpretation. How are we to understand his habit of eating with the wrong crowd? What are we to make of his seeming violations of the Sabbath? What was he doing when he overturned the tables of the money-changers in the temple? The meaning of such actions is hardly self-evident. Not surprisingly, different interpretations of the meaning and significance of these and other actions of Jesus have often led Christians to different conclusions about how best to follow him. Yet even when Christians have disagreed about some of theses details, most have agreed that Christians are called to pattern their lives after the character of Jesus as revealed through the stories of scripture.

One final point concerning the way character is revealed through story. If stories really are as central to understanding character as suggested

> **Stories are the primary way in which we make sense of our own lives and the lives of those around us.**

above, then it should come as no surprise that Jesus himself often used stories. Stories have a way of gripping our hearts and imaginations in ways that abstract discourse usually doesn't. Good stories, moreover, are memorable in ways that other forms of communication often are not. Jesus could have offered his hearers an elaborate theoretical discussion of the virtues of neighbor love; instead, he told the story of the Samaritan (Luke 10:30-37). Similarly, instead of presenting a philosophical discourse on the nature of God's love and mercy; he told the story of the prodigal son (Luke 15:11-32).

Perhaps all of the above will help us see that stories are rarely "just" stories, if by that we mean that stories are simply quaint ways of communicating what could just as easily be communicated by other means. On the contrary, stories are *the* primary way in which we make sense of our own lives and the lives of those around us.

Stories, stories, everywhere

As all of us are aware, scripture is not the only story around, nor are churches the only storytellers; rather, we are surrounded by powerful stories and storytellers. We are daily awash with voices telling us stories, offering to help us make sense of our lives. And as suggested above, these stories are never *just* stories, but are also invitations both to see ourselves and the world in a certain kind of way and to act in accordance with what we see.

For example, consider the different ways we are encouraged to think about ourselves and the world in light of the following kinds of stories:

- The stories that our families tell about what it means to be a Smith, an Escobar, or a Chen.

- The stories that teachers, politicians and talk-show hosts tell about what it means to be a responsible citizen.

- The stories that nearly everyone tells about how to be a good spouse, faithful friend, or reliable employee.

- The stories that parents, friends, movies, magazines, television and advertising tell about what it means to be "normal," "successful," or "beautiful."

- The stories that communities of faith tell about who God is, what God is doing in the world, and who we are in light of both.

That's a lot of different stories (and, of course, there are lots more), and not surprisingly, they all don't fit together neatly into a single, meaningful storyline. And so all of us, at least occasionally, find ourselves elevating some stories above others, making some stories more central to how we understand ourselves and reading the rest in light of that more central story. But how does one story become more central or more important than all the others? How does one story become *the* story through which we interpret all other stories?

Much as we may wish it were otherwise, there's likely no one way in which this happens. Some people intentionally choose to make a particular story the lens through which they read and understand all other stories; others probably feel more as though a particular story chose them; still others find themselves working this out on an almost daily basis. But regardless of how it happens, the point is that all of us find ourselves trying to make sense of ourselves and the world through certain stories that we have been told and which we subsequently retell ourselves and others.

So again, stories are never "just" stories. We don't just *tell* stories, but we understand our past, present and futures in terms of stories that we tell ourselves and which are told to us.

A Fishy Story

Consider this story, excerpted from the book, *A River Runs Through It:*

In our family, there was no clear line between religion and fly fishing. We lived at the junction of great trout rivers in western Montana, and our father was a Presbyterian minister and a fly fisherman who tied his own flies and taught others. He told us about Christ's disciples being fishermen, and we were left to assume, as my brother and I did, that all first-class fishermen on the Sea of Galilee were fly fisherman and that John, the favorite, was a dry-fly fisherman.

It is true that one day a week was given over wholly to religion. On Sunday mornings my brother, Paul, and I went to Sunday school and then to "morning services" to hear our father preach and in the evenings to Christian Endeavor and afterwards to "evening services" to hear our father preach again. In between on Sunday afternoons we had to study The Westminster Shorter Catechism *for an hour and then recite before we could walk the hills with him while he unwound between services. But he never asked us more than the first question in the catechism, "What is the chief end of man?" And we answered together so that one of us could carry on if the other forgot, "Man's chief end is to glorify God, and to enjoy Him forever." This always seemed to satisfy him, as indeed such a beautiful answer should have, and besides he was anxious to be on the hills where he could restore his soul and be filled again to overflowing for the evening sermon. His chief way of recharging himself was to recite to us from the sermon that was coming, enriched here and there with selections from the most successful passages of his morning sermon.*

Even so, in a typical week of our childhood Paul and I probably received as many hours of instruction in fly fishing as we did in all other spiritual matters.

After my brother and I became good fishermen, we realized that our father was not a great fly caster, but he was accurate and stylish and wore a glove on his casting hand. As he buttoned his glove in preparation to giving us a lesson, he would say, "It is an art that is performed on a four-count rhythm between ten and two o'clock."

After he buttoned his glove, he would hold his rod straight out in front of him, where it trembled with the beating of his heart. Always it was to be called a rod. If someone called it a pole, my father looked at him as a sergeant in the United States Marines would look at a recruit who had just called a rifle a gun.

My brother and I would have preferred to start learning how to fish by going out and catching a few, omitting entirely anything difficult or technical in the way of preparation that would take away from the fun. But it wasn't by way of fun that we were introduced to our father's art. If our father had had his say, nobody who did not know how to fish would be allowed to disgrace a fish by catching him.

My father was very sure about certain matters pertaining to the universe. To him, all good things—trout as well as eternal salvation—come by grace and grace comes by art and art does not come easy.

Norman Maclean, *A River Runs Through It*

The stories that we tell (and are told) about ourselves and our world are crucially important because they offer us whatever measure of coherence and meaning that we find in life. They do this in part by offering us ways in which to tie together many other elements of our lives. If, for example, we tell a certain story about who we are and what life is about, it will not be surprising if we try to live into that story by cultivating certain desires, convictions and dispositions, engaging in certain practices, and making use of the power inherent in certain institutions.

Thus, one of the ongoing challenges for any faith community is to sort through the role which stories play in its common life and in the lives of each disciple. What are the vital guiding stories that a community of faith tells about itself? What stories does it tell about where it has been and where it is going? How has this particular congregation or parish come to understand itself in light of the story of scripture?

It may very well be that a significant part of being a disciple of Jesus Christ is the willingness and skill to read one's life—and the life of one's community of faith—through the story of "God-with-us" revealed in scripture and the history of the church. May God continue to shape us more fully into the image of Christ as we continue to be open to the transforming power of the Spirit working through that story.

Scripture for Further Study

Scripture contains lots of stories, many of which reveal much about the character of God, the character of God's world, and the character of people in the stories (many of whom are remarkably like us!). Make a list here of biblical stories that you believe offer us such insight. For each story, jot down what you believe each story reveals about the character of God, the character of God's world, and/or the character of people like us.

Questions for Personal Reflection and Group Discussion

1. As you tell the story of your own life, who are the most significant people in that story? Why are these people so important in narrating who you are? What events in the course of your life do you tend to single out as most significant? Why have you come to see these as so important to who you are?

the expected birth
my brother's reaction

my husband

2. As you look to the future, what story do you see yourself living into? In other words, what story do you tell about where your life is going? How is this story about your future connected to the story you tell about your past?

one involving helping other people

3. How does your congregation or parish tell its story? Are there certain people or events that are taken as central to the story that you tell about yourselves? How and why have these people and events come to be central to your self-understanding as a community of faith?

the parish built as the mission church
    of Redeemer
+ then some R. people became members
What they did in Depression
what they did in 1968 + ??
by the time I joined ... all my criteria

4. As your faith community looks to the future, what story do you see yourselves living into? In other words, what story do you tell about where your congregation or parish is headed? How is this story about the future of your faith community connected to the story you tell about your past?

more engagement with community
    St. Thomas
    Raj.—   in Drexel Hill

5. What impact does the story of "God-with-us" as revealed in Scripture and the history of the church have on your own story and the story of your faith community? In what particular ways does this Biblical story inform or illuminate your own self-understanding or the identity of your community of faith?

Paying Greater Attention

1. In the coming days, work to pay particular attention to the stories that are told all around you (at work, in social settings, on television, etc.). In what ways are you encouraged to understand yourself and the world in light of these stories? In what ways are you encouraged to live into these stories?

2. Also work to pay attention in the coming days to the stories you tell yourself (and others) about who you are and why you do what you do. Note particularly those times when you are tempted to tell yourself (and others) a less-than-truthful story in order to alter the way you and your actions will likely be interpreted.

Conversation #6: Practices

Praise the LORD!
Praise God in his sanctuary;
    praise him in his mighty firmament!
Praise him for his mighty deeds;
  praise him according to his surpassing greatness!
Praise him with trumpet sound;
  praise him with lute and harp!
Praise him with tambourine and dance;
  praise him with strings and pipe!
Praise him with clanging cymbals;
  praise him with loud crashing cymbals!
Let everything that breathes praise the LORD!
Praise the LORD! *(Psalm 150)*

Remember the sabbath day, and keep it holy. Six days you shall labor and do all your work. But the seventh day is a sabbath to the LORD your God; you shall not do any work—you, your son or your daughter, your male or female slave, your livestock, or the alien resident in your towns. For six days the LORD made heaven and earth, the sea, and all that is in them, but rested the seventh day; therefore the LORD blessed the sabbath day and consecrated it. (Exodus 20:8-11)

When an alien resides with you in your land, you shall not oppress the alien. The alien who resides with you shall be to you as the citizen among you; you shall love the alien as yourself, for you were aliens in the land of Egypt: I am the Lord your God. (Leviticus: 19:33-34)

Be kind to one another, tenderhearted, forgiving one another, as God in Christ forgave you. (Ephesians 4:32)

Practicing faith

An important and potentially revolutionary shift is taking place in how many people think about the Christian faith. In the recent past, many Christians assumed that what primarily marked them *as* Christians was that they held certain beliefs. (To connect this to an earlier conversation, we might say that this way of identifying themselves as Christians was itself one of their central *convictions* about the Christian faith.) According to this way of thinking, a

Christian is someone who, for example, believes that Jesus was born of the virgin Mary, was the unique and only-begotten Son of God, was crucified to atone for our sins, and was resurrected by God on the third day. Not surprisingly, such an understanding of the Christian faith also led many to believe that what distinguished them from non-Christians (as well as from those in other Christian traditions) were primarily differences in what they believed.

As important as each of these beliefs are to the Christian faith, more and more Christians are rightly coming to see that beliefs alone do not define who they are as Christians. Equally central to their identity as Christians are certain *practices* of the Christian faith. Or perhaps put more accurately, practices are coming to be recognized as central to the Christian faith because practices are themselves best understood as a kind of "belief-in-action." Scripture is full of examples of such practices or "beliefs-in-action":

- Think of the many psalms or hymns found in scripture. It is one thing to believe intellectually that God is worthy of all praise; it is another to put that belief into practice by joyfully worshiping and offering God our praise.

- Consider God's commandment to keep the sabbath. Again, it is one thing to assent to the notion that God is sovereign and does not need our work to keep the world running; it is another to put that belief into practice by regularly resting from one's labors.

- Or recall God's instructions to ancient Israel concerning their treatment of aliens in their land. Once again, it is one thing to affirm that we were aliens in a strange land and that God took care of us; it's another to put that belief into practice *as the people of this God* by taking care of the strangers in our midst.

- Finally, it's one thing to assert that we have been forgiven by God; it's another to reflect the character of that God by putting this belief into action and forgiving those who have wronged us.

As these examples suggest, such practices serve both to express and reinforce basic convictions about who God is, what God has done, and who God has called us to be. But over generations, engaging in such practices becomes not just a means to express convictions but also a means by which these convictions are formed in others. Thus, children come to learn that this God is worthy of praise not only because they are told that this is so and they read it in scripture, but also because they are part of a community where this God is worshiped and praised. Or children come to learn that forgiveness is at the heart of the Christian faith not only because they are taught this or because they read it in scripture, but also because they are a part of a community where the practices of forgiveness and reconciliation are at the center of their common life.

But of course practices such as the ones listed above are not the only kinds that people engage in. Given that people hold a wide range of convictions and core beliefs, it's hardly surprising to discover that people engage in an equally wide range of practices or "beliefs-in-action." Nor is it likely surprising to discover that practices are not just bound up with convictions, but also with desires and dispositions. But to begin to see some of these connections and to see why any of this matters to discipleship, we need to back up once again and look more closely at the ways in which practices function in human life.

Practice, practice, practice

As noted above, when we speak of "practices" in this study we are referring to any of those activities in which we routinely engage that *presume* and *reinforce* a particular way of life (with all its accompanying desires, convictions, virtues, etc.). As a kind of "belief-in-action," practices flow from and bear witness to what people already believe about the world and their place in it, their desires and longings for the world and themselves, and the ways in which they are already disposed to interact in and with the world.

A relatively simple and mundane example may help clarify: the practice of washing your hands before a meal. The first and rather obvious thing to notice is that there's nothing "natural" about this practice; lots of people throughout history haven't done it and plenty of people in the world today still don't. In short, people who wash their hands before they eat do so not because it's natural to do so but because they have been formed over time to engage in this practice. The second thing to notice is that most of us no longer give much thought as to *why* we do it. At some point most of us either became convinced of the wisdom of hand-washing or gave in to the badgering of our parents and so developed habits of what we call "good hygiene." (We can leave for another time the practice and virtues of nail trimming!) Third, we should note that as children mature, they often come to understand better the reasons for hand-washing and so come to make this practice "their own" in the sense that they no longer see themselves as engaging in this practice primarily because their parents told them to.

> ***Practices are those activities in which we routinely engage that presume and reinforce a particular way of life.***

But how is the practice of hand-washing related to desires, convictions and virtues? One of the easiest ways to begin to see these connections is to ask yourself something like the following question: What assumptions would already have to be in place in order for this practice to seem perfectly sensible if not natural? In other words, because no action takes place in a cultural vacuum but always within a particular framework of cultural assumptions, what shared assumptions help to make this activity "fitting" or "appropriate"?

Again, let's stick with our relatively simple example of hand-washing and ask ourselves several questions about what is likely presumed and reinforced through engaging in this practice:

- What *desires* are presumed and reinforced by this practice? To name a few: the desire to be healthy and avoid illness; the desire to avoid spreading potentially harmful germs unnecessarily to others; the desire to be seen as cultured or civilized rather than as uncouth.

- What *convictions* are presumed and reinforced by this practice? Surely certain convictions about what counts for good health; convictions about the means and likelihood of spreading harmful diseases through inattention to hand-washing; and certain convictions about the effectiveness of hand-washing.

♦ What *dispositions* or *virtues* are presumed and reinforced by this practice? A few possibilities: the disposition to act in our own best interest; the disposition to be considerate of the health and well-being of others around us; the disposition to act in ways that gain the approval and admiration of those around us; the virtue of doing something even though its desired effects are not immediately apparent.

You should, of course, feel free to flesh out this picture further with other possibilities.

Finally, we should note that this practice is taught and reinforced by parents (and medical professionals) who tell stories of people who didn't practice "good hygiene" and who became terribly sick. These stories, coupled with the above framework and our own sense of who our society holds up for commendation, go a long way toward giving us good reasons to wash our hands regularly.

The point here, of course, is not to criticize either the practice of hand-washing or the assumptions underwritten by such a practice. The only objective at this point is to see the way in which engaging in a particular practice reinforces a whole range of things, many of which we may not even be conscious of at the time. This is one of the primary reasons it's important to pay attention to the practices in which we engage. If something as simple as the practice of regularly washing your hands presumes and reinforces a whole set of desires, convictions and dispositions, then it's quite possible that we are also daily being formed by all kinds of other practices in which we engage but to which we pay very little attention.

Formative practices

Of course the practices that are most formative of who we are tend to be considerably more complicated than hand-washing. To see this, take some time to reflect on the following list of everyday practices and see if you are able to discern some of the desires, convictions and dispositions (as well as virtues and vices) that each practice likely nourishes:

Making promises

Planting and tending a garden

Engaging in conversation

Watching television

Saying you're sorry

Praying

Writing letters to a friend

Singing a hymn with others

Playing competitive sports

Shopping for the latest fashions

Taking walks in the woods or a park

Recycling a newspaper

Voting in an election

Visiting the elderly and the sick

Taking a vacation

Reading the Bible

Sharing a meal

Playing games with children

What becomes immediately obvious after reading such a list is that people do these things (or don't do them) for lots of different reasons. (The same is also true even of hand-washing. If you doubt this, go back and read about Jesus' run-in with the scribes and Pharisees over hand-washing in Matthew 15.) This suggests that there's no reason to believe that there's only one set of desires, convictions and dispositions that are presumed and reinforced by the above practices. Each of the above practices—as well as nearly any practice that we could identify—could flow from very different ways of life. This observation has at least two important implications.

First, it suggests that two people who look like they're doing "the same thing" may be better understood —at least for the reasons we care about here—as doing something very different. For example, a person who engages in a conversation primarily to hear his own voice is not doing the same thing as someone who engages in a conversation primarily to learn from another's perspective. Similarly, a person who reads the Bible because she enjoys reading ancient texts is not doing the same thing as someone who reads it fully expecting to be led by God. In short, the reasons we engage in a particular practice shape its formative effects.

This helps us see why it's never enough to simply look to see if a particular practice is being engaged in, since in most cases that alone will likely reveal very little. What is always more important—and harder to get a handle on—is why a group of people engages in a particular practice in the first place. What does a particular group of people believe they are doing by engaging in a particular practice? This is only one reason why it's probably not particularly illuminating to count the number of people who engage in

> **The reasons we engage in a particular practice shape its formative effects.**

the practice of "going to church" each week, since what these people understand themselves to be doing varies so greatly that it hardly makes sense to say that they are engaging in the same practice.

This leads directly to the second implication: the variety of *reasons* for engaging in a practice likely lead to different *ways* of engaging in and evaluating a practice. A young man, for example, who regularly works out at the gym, sculpting his body in hopes of attracting a particular female, will likely engage in this practice (and evaluate its effectiveness) differently from one who exercises in response to a recent life-threatening heart attack. Similarly, a woman who prays primarily to persuade God to give her what she desires is likely to engage in prayer differently (and evaluate its effectiveness differently) than someone who understands prayer primarily as aligning one's own desires with God's.

All of this taken together suggests that potentially formative practices cannot be examined in isolation from the wider frameworks in which they are practiced. Engaging in particular practices, in other words, neither mechanically nor magically guarantees a particular outcome. This is one more reason why the stories we tell are so important, since the frameworks within which practices "make sense" and do their formative work are nearly always "story-shaped" frameworks.

A "Practical" Example

In one local church the congregation found that local children were turning up an hour or more before the service, looking for company, entertainment, or mischief. For a few years two members of the congregation opened the doors an hour before the service began and tried to offer a mixture of conversation, education, and encouragement, together with a little bit of discipline. Slowly they began to notice that one explanation for the children's behavior was that they were hungry. So a pattern began of holding a breakfast 45 minutes before the service began, and during that time weaving into the conversation some high and low points in the week, encouragements and discouragements to faith, and hopes and fears for the near future. Gradually this breakfast extended so that it became not just for the children but for the whole congregation: and three or four times a year instead of breakfast everyone would set about getting ready for a celebratory lunch that would follow the service, and would be made up of contributions, great and small, from almost every member. Thus were human need and a point of aggravation transformed into an occasion of celebration, fellowship, and grace. The need of the human body became an experience of the body of Christ.

Samuel Wells, God's Companions (Wiley-Blackwell, 2006)

In this brief account we glimpse something of how practices are always situated in broader frameworks, since the decision to begin a breakfast for these children was rooted in a whole set of convictions, stories, and other practices having to do with scripture's call to welcome the stranger and the church's experience of being fed at the Lord's Table by a generous and hospitable God.

Practices matter

Because practices inevitably involve action, it's important to note that in addition to forming us to act in certain ways in certain situations, every culture also tells us what will count for acting in the first place. In other words, every culture shapes us to think of certain things as "doing nothing." So, for example, if people in our day read Jesus' words about how we should respond when someone strikes us on the right cheek (Matt. 5:39), our "natural" response, given the way we've been formed, is to ask, "But why does Jesus insist that I do nothing?" Of course, Jesus may not be asking us to "do nothing," but to do the *harder* thing, which if you've ever done it, sure feels like you're doing "something." A similar observation could be made with regard to the practice of prayer, which many of us have come to think of as "not really doing anything."

Trying to get a handle on the ways in which practices form us is not easy. If it's any consolation, consider working through this material as itself a kind of practice—the practice of thinking hard about matters that matter. Such a practice has its own rewards, though they rarely come quickly or easily. Pray that as you continue to think on these things and discuss them with others that God will help you see the ways in which the practices we engage in every day either help to fashion us more closely into the image of Christ or help to mold us into an image far less glorious.

Questions for Personal Reflection and Group Discussion

1. What practices do you regularly engage in that likely shape your view of the world and your place in it, your desires and longings, and your character? Take one of these specific practices and trace the possible connections between it and your convictions, desires and character. What story do you tell about why you engage in this practice and how does this story affect the ways you engage in it?

2. What do you think are some of the core practices at the center of your congregation's life together? To get at this, you might try filling in the following blank: "If we as a congregation or parish stopped [doing] _____, we would stop being who we are."

3. Once you have identified what you think are some of these core practices, reflect further on them by asking yourself the following: How have each of these practices been nourished over time by our congregation? How have each of these practices changed over time here?

Paying Greater Attention

If it's true that all of us are shaped more than we know by engaging in all kinds of everyday practices, perhaps it would be a good idea to attend to these more consciously. In the coming days and weeks, pay greater attention to 1) the kinds of practices that you engage in regularly; and 2) some of the specific ways that these likely shape you. Jot down some of your reflections on these matters here.

Conversation #7: Institutions

> *"You shall observe this rite as a perpetual ordinance for you and your children. When you come to the land that the L*ORD *will give you, as he has promised, you shall keep this observance. And when your children ask you, 'What do you mean by this observance?' you shall say, 'It is the passover sacrifice to the L*ORD*, for he passed over the houses of the Israelites in Egypt, when he struck down the Egyptians but spared our houses.'" (Exodus 12:24-27)*
>
> *"The sabbath was made for humankind, and not humankind for the sabbath." (Mark 2:27)*
>
> *For I received from the Lord what I also handed on to you, that the Lord Jesus on the night when he was betrayed took a loaf of bread, and when he had given thanks, he broke it and said, "This is my body that is broken for you. Do this in remembrance of me." In the same way he took the cup also, after supper, saying, "This cup is the new covenant in my blood. Do this, as often as you drink it, in remembrance of me." For as often as you eat this bread and drink the cup, you proclaim the Lord's death until he comes. (1 Cor. 11:23-26)*

When you hear the word "institution," what images come to your mind? Do you find the associations conjured by this word largely positive or negative? If you're like a lot of folks in contemporary society, you are somewhat suspicious, if not distrustful, about the role of institutions in human life and the power that they often wield. Some of this distaste may spring from what you regard as the "impersonal" character of institutions, while some of your aversion may spring from a deep reservoir of stories that all of us can tell about corrupt, coercive, and oppressive institutions. Indeed, many people held up as heroes in our collective memory—Galileo Galilei, George Washington, Abraham Lincoln, Martin Luther King, Jr., Rosa Parks—are typically regarded *as* heroes precisely because they stood up against unjust and oppressive institutions. We also hear echoes of this suspicion of institutions when people in our day claim that they consider themselves to be "spiritual" but have little interest in or respect for the so-called "institutional church."

Dealing head-on with our bias

All of which is to say, if many of us have a bias against institutions, we probably come by it honestly, for our imaginations have been formed in a culture that is often deeply suspicious of institutions. Yet this is only part of the story. The rest of the story is this: whether we acknowledge it or not, our daily lives are shaped and ordered—often for the better—by countless institutions.

In what follows we will be using a rather broad definition of "institution." For our purposes in this conversation, an institution is any organization or social structure that orders life for a particular group of people. In addition to those organizations we typically think of when we think of institutions, this broader definition includes such things as agencies, laws, traditions, programs, policies, even committees! As such, institutions are brought into being and sustained in order to serve (and preserve) a particular way of life that people regard as good and therefore worthy of being sustained. Or said in another way, at their best institutions enable the passing down of wisdom, knowledge, and a way of life from one generation to another. To remind ourselves of how this works, let us consider a brief list of some of the contemporary institutions that directly and indirectly shape our lives:

- Educational institutions: schools, colleges, universities, accrediting associations, libraries

- Political institutions: political offices, elections, rule of law, founding documents (constitutions, etc.)

- Legal institutions: legislatures, laws, courts, police departments, prisons

- Medical institutions: hospitals, medical schools, insurance regulations

- Social and cultural institutions: marriage, family, language, holidays, traditions, museums, entertainment industries

- Economic institutions: businesses and industries, currencies, banks, stock and bond markets, labor unions, regulatory agencies

At least four important things become obvious by reviewing such a list. First, every institution is itself the result of shared convictions concerning what is important in human life. For example, it's precisely because a large number of people share certain convictions about the relationship between knowledge, its dissemination, and the public good that we have such institutions as public libraries.

Second, the boundaries between different categories of institution listed above (educational, legal, medical, etc.) are relatively arbitrary and fluid, since many of these institutions could easily be placed in more than one category. For instance, the entertainment industry functions both as a social and an economic institution, and arguably as an educational one as well. (For those wondering about the absence of so-called "religious institutions" from the list, rest assured that this omission was intentional. See question #3 below.)

Third, despite the bias that many of us have against institutions, it's difficult to imagine human life without them. In fact, it's not clear that humans could do without institutions even if we wanted to. We seem drawn to creating structures that seek to bring order out of chaos.

And finally, it's not clear that we *should* want to do without institutions, for despite their shortcomings and potential for being twisted to false purposes (more about that in a moment), institutions make possible both order and cooperation within and across generations that few of us would be willing (or wise) to give up.

So at the end of the day, regardless of whatever reservations (justified or otherwise) we might have about institutions, most of us are probably glad that there are laws about which side of the street to drive on and disincentives known as fines for breaking those laws. Most of us are likely appreciative that there are hospitals to care for our loved ones and agencies that regulate what can be put in our food and drinking water. And most of us are probably grateful that we can read these chapters and reflect on them seriously as a result of having been schooled in the art of reading and thinking carefully.

The purpose of institutions

Although institutions and structures come into existence in lots of different ways, they almost always take the form they do as a concrete way of supporting and sustaining certain sets of practices, desires, convictions and the like. For example, people throughout history have thought it important to educate their young, though the means and structures they have employed to accomplish this have varied widely. Local public school systems represent one particular set of structures and institutions for seeking to carry out this desired task, but they hardly represent the only option. Nevertheless, whatever structures or institutions are employed will reflect and instill a whole set of desires, convictions, dispositions and practices. And more than likely, all of these together will be justified by a particular story or set of stories that "makes sense" of educating children in this way.

> *Institutions make possible both order and cooperative behavior within and across generations that few of us would be willing (or wise) to give up.*

Thus, one of the reasons we have left to last the issue of institutions in our discussion of formation is not because they are less important than the other aspects, but because institutions make so little sense *apart* from the other aspects. In other words, institutions are structures that in various ways (directly and indirectly) flow out of, instill and support certain sets of desires, convictions, virtues, stories and practices. For these reasons, *institutions are inherently formative in character.*

Take, for example, any institution you can think of. (You might pick one or two from the lists above.) To understand this institution *as* an institution, and to see how its function is inherently formative, consider each of the following questions:

- What desires are met, instilled and validated in and through this institution (and the practices it supports)?

- What convictions do people hold that would lead them to believe that such an institution is necessary or at least desirable? What agreed-upon and shared purposes does it supposedly serve?

- What dispositions, inclinations and virtues (and perhaps vices) does this institution nurture, both intentionally and unintentionally?

- What stories are told about why this institution exists and why it has the current shape it does?

♦ What practices is this institution designed to support and make possible? How does the current shape of this institution influence how these practices are practiced?

Whatever sense we make of institutions, therefore, cannot be easily separated from the sense we make of all these other aspects of our lives. Moreover, as noted above, whatever hesitation or suspicion we may have about institutions cannot be linked simply to their character as institutions, for as such they support and maintain much of what we rightly care about.

So what is it about institutions that makes us so nervous?

A life of their own

Anyone who has had to deal with institutions knows that in at least one respect most of them are very much like ocean liners: they're hard to turn on a dime. In other words, institutions can change course, but not easily and typically not very quickly. For this reason alone, institutions tend to be conservative in nature. This does, of course, have a positive side: by their very character as institutions, these structures are bigger than—and therefore outside the easy control or manipulation of—solitary individuals. But there can often be a downside to this as well. Over time, institutions can begin to take on a life of their own, often independent of the purposes they were brought into existence to serve. When this happens, people often end up caring more deeply about preserving certain institutional structures than about whether these structures still serve the purposes for which they were created.

For example, the school calendar still widely used in many school districts across the country, which gives students two or three months off in the summer, was instituted long ago when many families were involved in agriculture and needed their children home to help during the busy growing season. Since that time, much has changed, and a number of educators have argued for instituting a new school calendar that would be tied more closely to educational purposes and to what is for many people a vastly different cultural context. But as the debate across the country has shown, changing an institutional form like the school calendar is no easy task. The reason is obvious: even though most children are no longer directly involved in agriculture, the rhythm of their lives has been formed by a calendar that was instituted as though they were. Over time, people began to think of the summer months less as a time for farming and more as a time for family vacations. As a result, the school calendar now serves different purposes than it was designed to serve.

Whether those purposes are just as worthy of being served, or whether some other purposes ought to take center stage, is really what the current debate is about.

> *People often end up caring more deeply about preserving certain institutional structures than about whether these structures still serve the purposes for which they were created.*

Of course, concerns about institutions taking on a life of their own are nothing new. For example, Jesus himself seemed to have had his own concerns regarding the institution of the sabbath. According to scripture, God had instituted the sabbath to provide rest from the toil and anxiety of everyday life. By the time of Jesus, however, the sabbath had taken on a life of its own. Indeed, the purpose of the sabbath seemed to have been turned on its head: rather than the sabbath serving people, people were now serving the sabbath by devoting enormous amounts of energy trying to follow all the well-intentioned rules designed to help people know whether or not they were "keeping" the sabbath. One of the unintended consequences was that many people couldn't wait for the sabbath to be over so that they wouldn't have to be so anxious about whether they were violating the sabbath rules. So rather than being a respite from toil and anxiety, the sabbath had become a new source of both!

It's tempting for us to look at this situation and assure ourselves that we would never do something like that. But are we so sure? Each of us are likely being shaped by institutions that seem so "natural" in their current form, so much a part of the fabric of everyday life as we have come to experience it, that we have long ago stopped (or perhaps never even started) asking about what purposes such institutions were supposed to serve. For example, one prominent social critic in our day has asked, "What's an economy for?" as a way of trying to generate a national discussion about what purposes an institution like the economy is supposed to serve. Another social critic has asked similar questions about public education, suggesting that what we most need in our country is not a debate about national testing or putting more computers in classrooms but a frank and honest discussion about the purposes that public education is supposed to serve.

So what's the church for?

Perhaps it's also time for followers of Jesus in our day to ask similar questions about the church and its institutional form and structures. Lots of people now offer proposals for how to "do" church better, but perhaps what is most needed is a frank and open discussion about God's purpose for the church. Does it really make sense to evaluate these various contemporary proposals for doing church better apart from examining the purposes the church is supposed to serve? Do we know what those purposes are? Do we know whether or to what extent our faith community as it is currently organized is fulfilling those purposes?

These and other questions concerning the identity and mission of the church will be at the heart of our next series of conversations, "The Shape of God's Reign." But for now a couple of things can be said as we anticipate these future discussions. First, the church is often described as a collection of people who have something in common called Christian faith and who get together regularly to share it with each other and to communicate it to those "outside." This understanding of the church may seem reasonable to us; it seems, after all, to offer a clearly-articulated purpose. But such an understanding does not do justice to the New Testament's vision of the church (*ekklesia* in Greek), for in the Bible we learn that the church is not so much a host site for like-minded individuals as it is a space or place where we can *see* properly—God, God's creation, and ourselves—and where we act as sign and witness to God's redemptive purposes for the world. In his well-known book *Life Together*, German theologian Dietrich Bonhoeffer rightly insisted that the church "is not an ideal which we must realize; it is rather a reality created by God in Christ in which we may participate." Understood this way, the church is not an "institution" to be managed by smart people but a communion across time and space whose purpose is to worship and bear witness to this

God and no other. What such an understanding of the church might mean for the shape of our everyday lives will be the burden of our next study.

Questions for Personal Reflection and Group Discussion

1. Reflect once again on the shape of your daily life. What structures and institutions influence the shape of your daily life? In what specific ways do these structures and institutions exert their influence? Where are you thankful for the ordering and influence that these structures bring? Where (and why) are you frustrated by these structures and institutions?

church
health care institutions
structures of scholarship
academe

2. Because institutions can easily begin to serve purposes other than the ones for which they were brought into being, it may be wise to evaluate them periodically, not out of some naïve desire to discard them, but to determine whether such structures and institutions are actually serving the purposes we want them to serve. If they are not, these structures and institutions likely need to be reformed or replaced by others that will serve the desired purposes. As you've thought about institutions in light of this conversation, what examples have you come up with of institutions or structures that may have taken on a life of their own and now no longer serve the purposes for which they were brought into being?

the tenuring process ?? I think, to assure freedom of inquiry but what about like rest of profess. related work force?
the complexity of health care system — insurance systems — wouldn't it be simpler if we had a Medicare for all? or a NHS ??
R.C. Church — that's easy!
Episcopal Church ? — not questioning source of the money people give in donations.

3. Not only does every culture order the lives of its citizens by means of certain institutions (such as legal and economic structures), but every culture also forms us to understand the relationship among different institutions in certain kinds of ways. So, for example, in our day the church is widely believed to be an institution charged with addressing the "religious" or "spiritual" concerns of its members as opposed to their educational, economic, legal or political concerns, which are handled by other institutions in our society. What do you see as the advantages and disadvantages of this "division of labor"?

not good to be so divided

4. Reflect on the institutional structure of your faith community and the broader church structures of which it is a part. In your view, where do the current institutional structures foster genuine growth and discipleship? How specifically do they accomplish this? Where, in your view, do they possibly (and no doubt unintentionally) inhibit growth and discipleship? Can you imagine different structures or institutions that might better serve the purposes of the church as you understand them?

Paying Greater Attention

1. Try to be more mindful in the coming weeks of all the many ways in which structures and institutions (including all kinds of organizations, agencies, programs and traditions) shape and influence—for good and ill—your everyday life and the lives of those around you. Jot down some of your thoughts in the space below.

2. Over the past several weeks you've hopefully become more attuned to the shape of your life both as a person and as a faith community. What have you become more aware of over these weeks that you think is most significant? What do you want to continue to pay particular attention to in the coming weeks?

Made in the USA
Middletown, DE
01 August 2020